MW01671007

Cynthia [illegible],

Thank you for all your help here at New Life International.

God bless you,

Yvonne McGuire

Published by,
Yvonne E. McGuire
6764 South Bloomington Trail
Underwood, IN 47177

www.henrylorentzen.com

ISBN # 978-0-9852198-3-3

First Printing 2500 December 2013

Artwork by Henry Lorentzen & Yvonne Lorentzen McGuire
Designer - Stephanie DeBoer, DeBoer Creative, LLC.

Printed by
L & D Mail Masters, Inc.
110 Security Parkway
New Albany, Indiana 47150
1-(812) 981-7161

Printed in the U.S.A.

Homestead Memories on the *Buffalo Paunch Creek*

The Story of North Dakota Pioneers, Lorentz and Martha Lorentzen and Family.

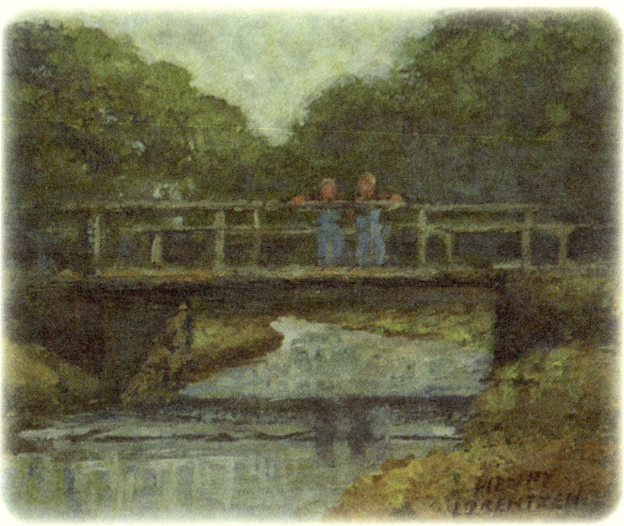

Told by their granddaughter,

YVONNE LORENTZEN MCGUIRE

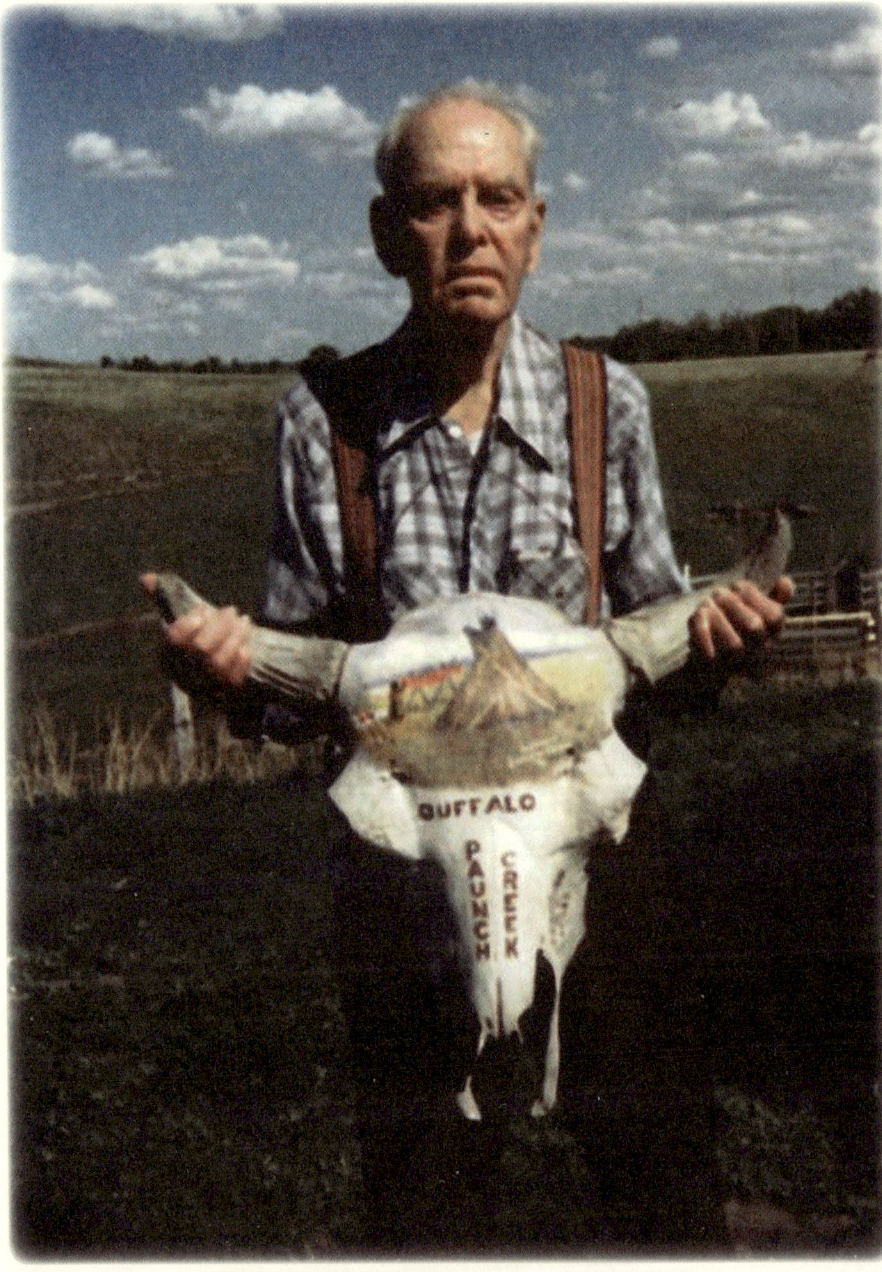

HENRY LORENTZEN HOLDING BUFFALO SKULL
FOUND AT BUFFALO PAUNCH CREEK
PAINTED BY HIM IN THE 1980'S.

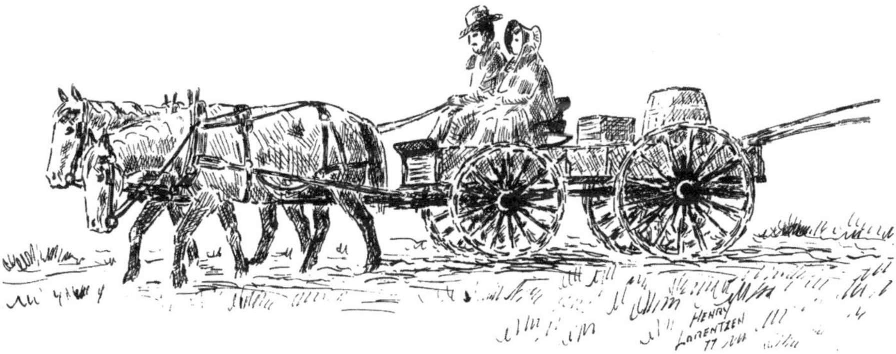

Dedicated to the memory of:

My brave North Dakota Pioneer Grandmother,
Martha Helena (Thompson) Lorentzen
(March 19, 1867 – March 6, 1956)

and to:

My adventuresome Norwegian Grandfather
whom I never had the privilege of knowing
Lorentz Lorentzen
(June 29, 1850 – November 10, 1906)

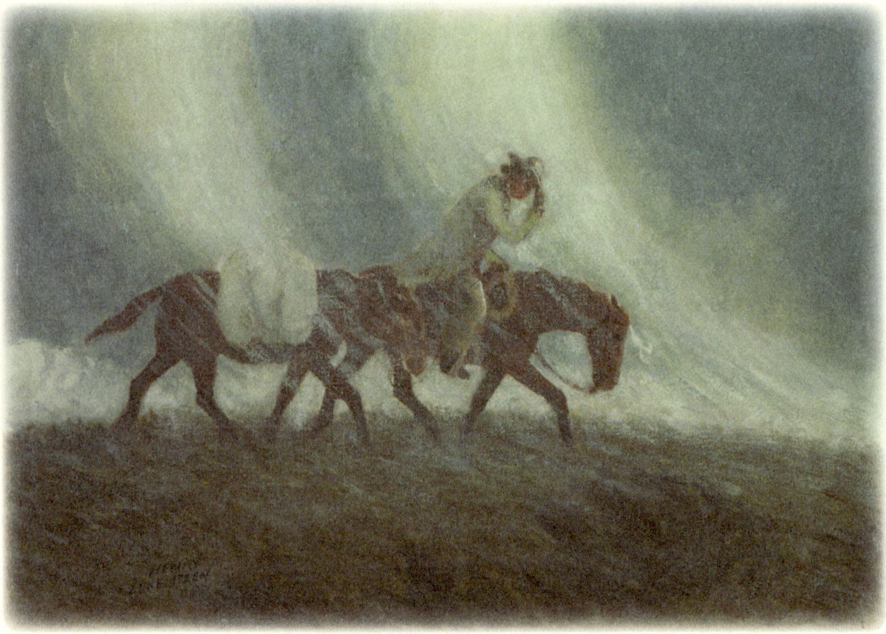

"RIDING OUT THE STORM"
OIL PAINTING BY HENRY LORENTZEN

-Table of Contents-

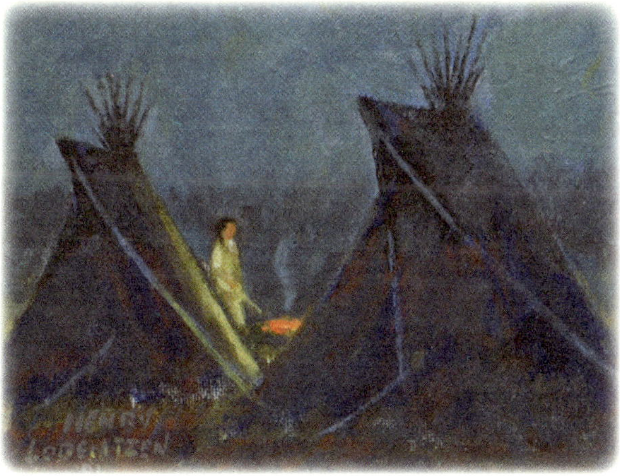

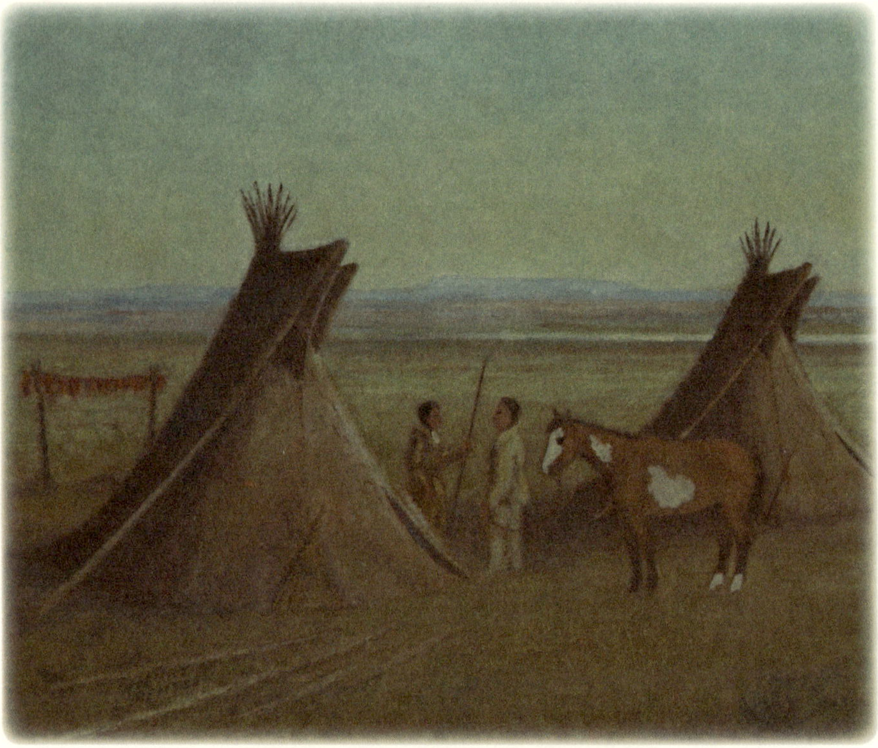

OIL PAINTING BY HENRY LORENTZEN
IN THE 1970'S.

Foreword

Mysterious and complex mathematical calculations in an off-limits drawer ... strange and complicated brass instruments ... a carefully framed needlepoint sampler with the motto saying "Knowledge is Power" ... a weathered log wall adorned with a masterpiece painting of a majestic Norwegian sailing ship ... these, and more were some of the treasures within a humble homestead cabin along the Missouri River in the middle of North Dakota. What were these things? Where did they come from? Who were these people?

When I was a kid, I visited the homestead once before the fire. My memories are a blur and tainted by an angry goose that guarded the yard and threatened to eat me. So why would Mom write a book entitled: "Homestead Memories on the Buffalo Paunch Creek"? To better know the answers to this question, you will want to know something about the people and the stories wrapped inside other stories. You are about to see "art" in a new light. Art on canvas tries to capture a three-dimensional world and expression within a two-dimensional frame. While Mom is an artist, here she uses a media other than paints, chalk, watercolors, and canvas. Using the media of "words" Mom has artistically painted in multiple-dimensions without the constraints of two-dimensional canvases.

In our fast paced world - flooded with social media and gibberish text messages, our society has lost much of the art of - let's face it, "REAL communication". We are losing the art of conversation, storytelling, conceptualizing, empathizing, and even the art of listening! As such, we often miss the story within the story, miss the deeper meanings, and fail to slow down and reflect upon where we came from or prayerfully consider where we might be going. Woven throughout this book is the connecting theme that small things or seemingly insignificant decisions really do matter. They matter most when we reshape the future by reflecting upon them and remember from where we have come.

There are many branches in the road of life, and very seldom can we explore both forks in a road, if ever. As my father Byron once told me, "Life is like a coin, you can spend it any way you want, but you can only spend it once". This book is about people; it is about their lives; and it is about the decisions they made along the way often in the face of circumstances pressed upon them by fate and tragedy. Decisions and events really do have consequences. The stories of this book illustrate this truth and that life and death often hang in the balance by the decisions we make … and they reshape the future. It is also about us; today we are part of the future!

On a personal level, I recall hearing many wonderful, as well as tragic stories, several times while growing up. As I was reading Mom's final draft in preparation for writing this "Foreward", a revelation occurred to me. Growing up with the identity of being the Great-Great-Grandson of Captain Emanuel Lorentzen has helped shape who I am. One such story was the tragic death of Elizabeth, his infant granddaughter to cholera in 1885 and her lost grave in Chicago. Might this story have been a subtle behind the scenes influence upon the water purification ministry of New Life International today?

Mom has artistically taken us on a road less traveled and "painted" a panorama that grapples with the troubling truth: there might not be any "insignificant decisions" in life … every decision and event has consequences for the future and eternity, and to what or to Whom do we turn for guidance?

Byron Duvon McGuire
CEO New Life International Inc. www.WaterForTheWorld.com

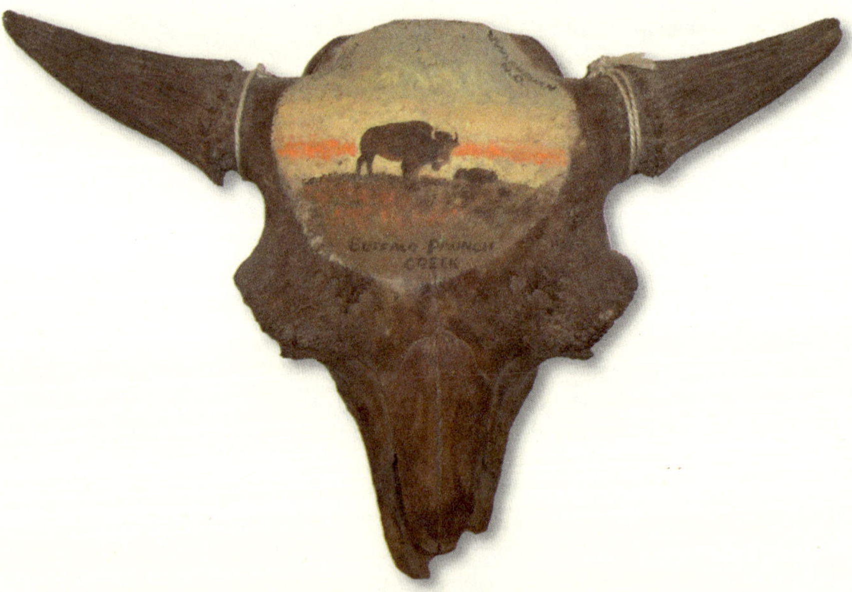

ANCIENT SKULL FOUND IN THE BUFFALO PAUNCH CREEK
PAINTING BY HENRY LORENTZEN
(Owned by Byron Duvon McGuire)

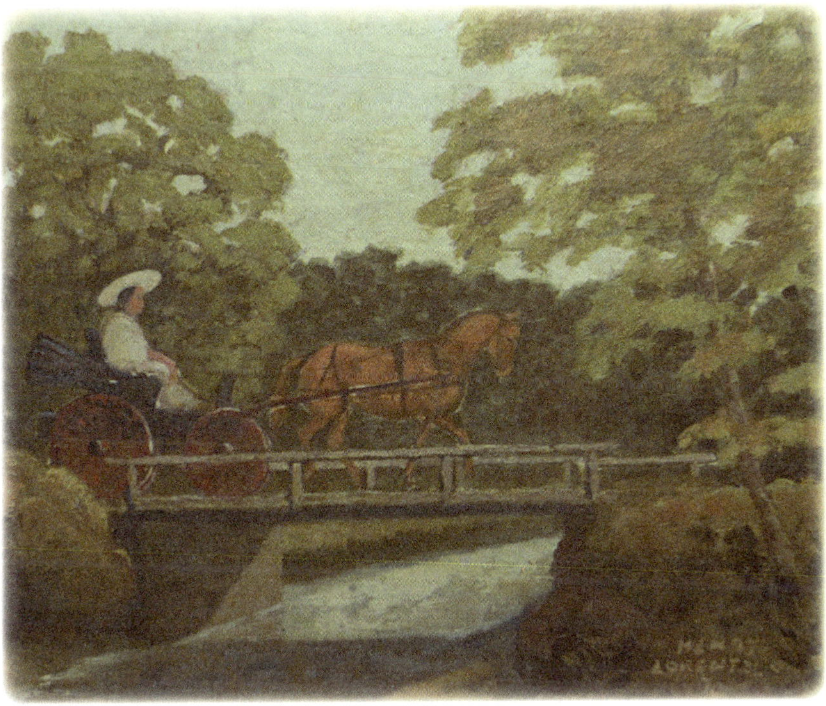

BRIDGE OVER BUFFALO PAUNCH CREEK
OIL PAINTING BY HENRY LORENTZEN

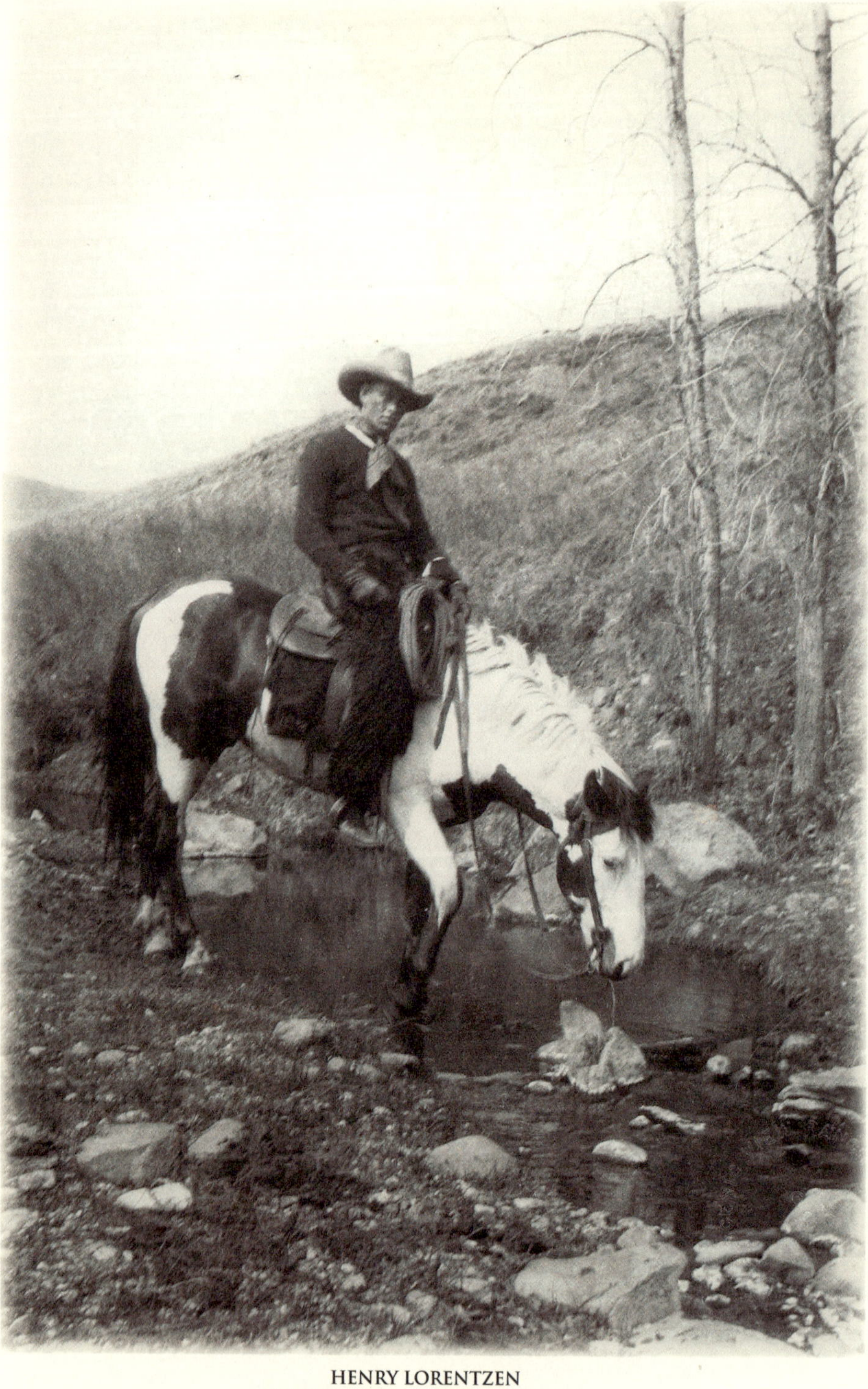

HENRY LORENTZEN
AT THE BUFFALO PAUNCH CREEK
LATE 1920'S

Author's Note

The old homestead cabin on the Buffalo Paunch Creek and Grandma Martha played an important part in my life. I named my first daughter Martha, and my cousin Lorentz also named a daughter Martha. I have wanted to share with my children, grandchildren, my nieces and nephews, and others some memories they otherwise might not know about. We have a wonderful heritage that we can pass on to future generations. This collection of memories is not intended to be a complete historical account of the Lorentzen family, and their descendants, but it is based on my personal experiences--what I have seen or heard firsthand. Other family members, I'm sure, have their own special memories.

My artist father Henry Lorentzen used to recite the following poem, which encourages us to not bemoan missed opportunities, but to believe that opportunity comes again to give us another chance.

OPPORTUNITY

Walter Malone (1866-1915)

"They do me wrong who say I come no more
When once I knock and fail to find you in;
For every day I stand outside your door
And bid you wake, and rise to fight and win.

Wail not for precious chances passed away!
Weep not for golden ages on the wane!
Each night I burn the records of the day –
At sunrise every soul is born again!"

I challenge you, the reader, to treasure your own heritage and to learn all you can about it. Opportunity is knocking at your door. You have memories to share with your family and future generations to follow. We in our daily lives are making memories for others to recall someday. I pray we will leave behind good memories.

Yvonne McGuire

6764 South Bloomington Trail
Underwood, IN 47177

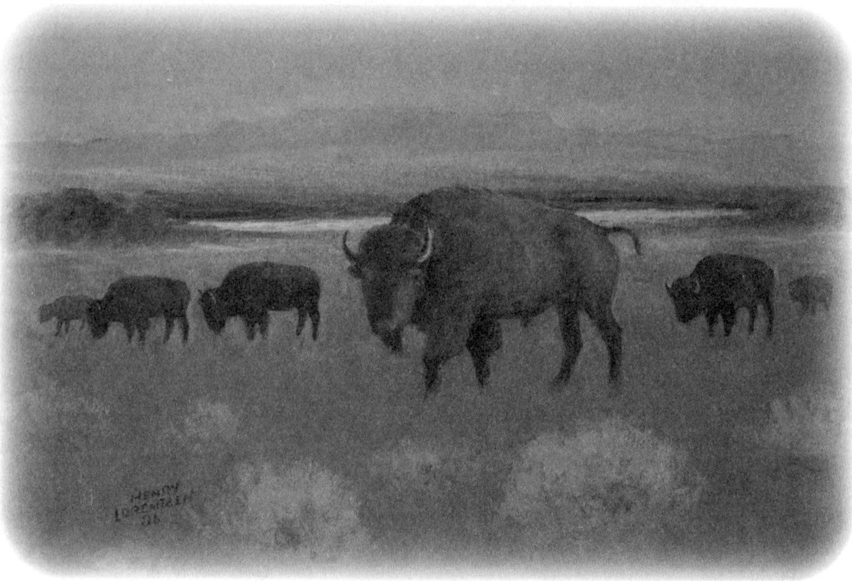

OIL PAINTING BY HENRY LORENTZEN
1986

CHAPTER 1

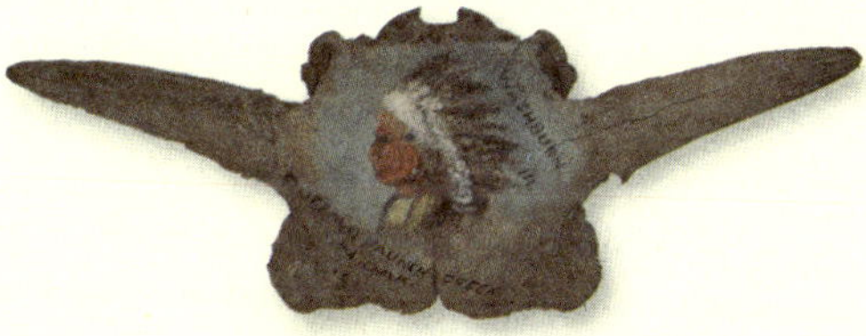

Legend of Buffalo Paunch Creek

Over fifty years have passed since I last stepped over the threshold and entered the old log homestead cabin of my Grandmother Martha Lorentzen. This cabin was my father Henry's boyhood home in North Dakota situated not far from the Missouri River, west of Washburn, near where the Lewis and Clark expedition spent the winter of 1804-1805.

The log cabin, shop, granary, barn, and corrals were built on a flat bench of land overlooking the Missouri River and wooded bottom land to the south. High hills covered with prairie grass rising behind on the north provided shelter and merged with more distant hills to the west and east. In the deep coulee between the hills, the steadily flowing Buffalo Paunch Creek wound its way twisting and turning around clumps of wild fruit bushes and trees, cutting its way through dirt banks strewn with scattered glacial stones and boulders on its way to join the Missouri. My father, Henry, said the creek was a refuge when prairie fires swept the area. It provided spawning pools for varied fish, a home for the muskrat, and a natural haven for the teal and other kinds of water fowl.

The creek was a favorite place for childhood explorations of my brothers, Norman and Ross, my sister,

Estell, and me. We called it Grandma's Creek or "crick" as we likely pronounced it. How exciting and rewarding it was to discover buffalo skulls washed out of the creek banks. Because of the number of skulls and occasional bones found in the creek over the years, we speculated that perhaps an Indian hunting party in hot pursuit had stampeded a herd of buffalo off the north cliff into the creek. Huge herds of buffalo, hundreds of years before, had worn a deep path from the hills down into the coulee to drink at the creek. Down one steep hill in the pasture, there still remains a deeply eroded path where the buffalo used to travel single file. Today, horses and cattle follow the same path down to the creek to slake their thirst.

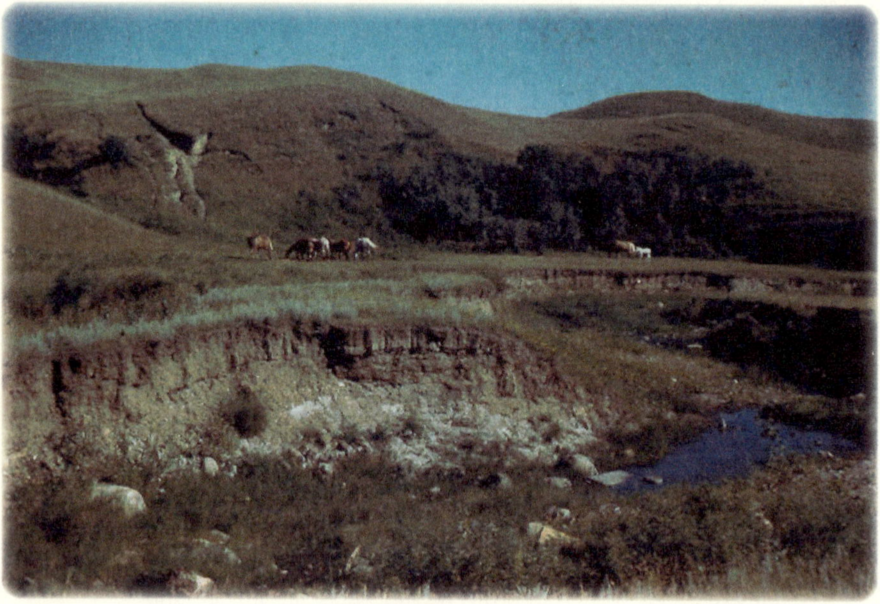

Many years ago my father told me a legend or old story of a large encampment of Indians in this vicinity. While I've been unable to trace the source or accuracy of it, I came across a notebook of my father's in which he began to write in 1985 this unfinished story:

> *"Approximately four-hundred years ago a large band of Arikara Indians were encamped at the mouth of a creek where it emptied into the Missouri. At this point the river has run in an east and west direction through the centuries, and it was on the north bank of the river about two and a half miles above the steep banks where the town of Washburn is now located. The sheltered flats were a natural camping area."*

From my memory I will continue the story: It was an unusually severe winter with deep snows and bitterly cold temperatures. There was a scarcity of food with the Indians close to starvation. Wild game in the area such as deer and buffalo had already been killed or the few remaining had moved elsewhere in search of food or shelter. Finally, one buffalo was located by a hunting party, killed, and dressed out.

The younger members of the tribe, under leadership of a rising young warrior, received the entrails and paunch, or stomach of the buffalo. The older members, under leadership of their old chief, received the actual meat of the carcass. A disagreement over this division of the buffalo meat resulted in the younger group breaking away from the old Arikara tribe and following their leader to form a new tribe which became known as the Hidatsa. Thereafter, where this momentous decision was made, the creek became known as the Buffalo Paunch Creek.

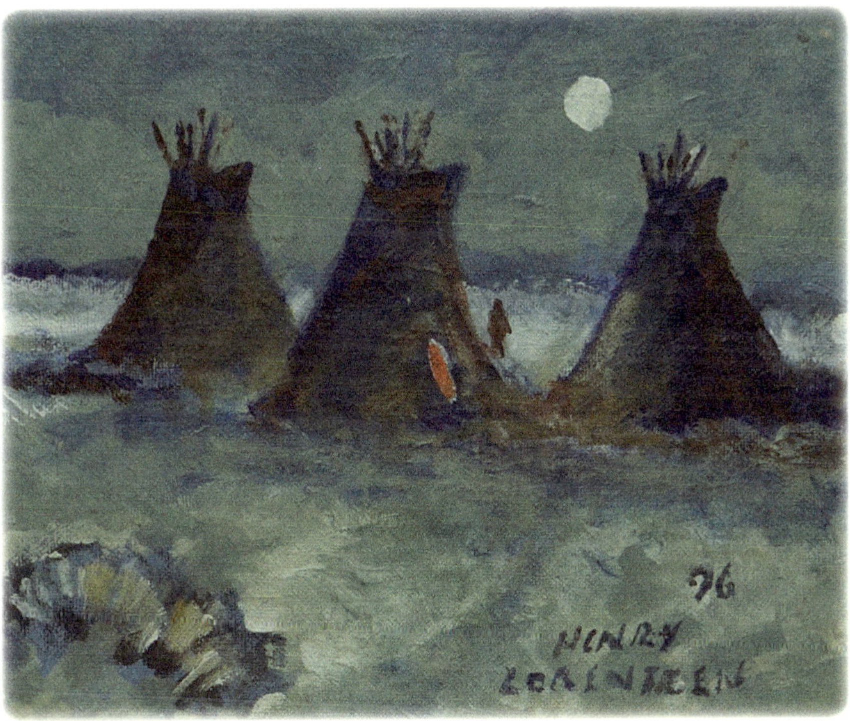

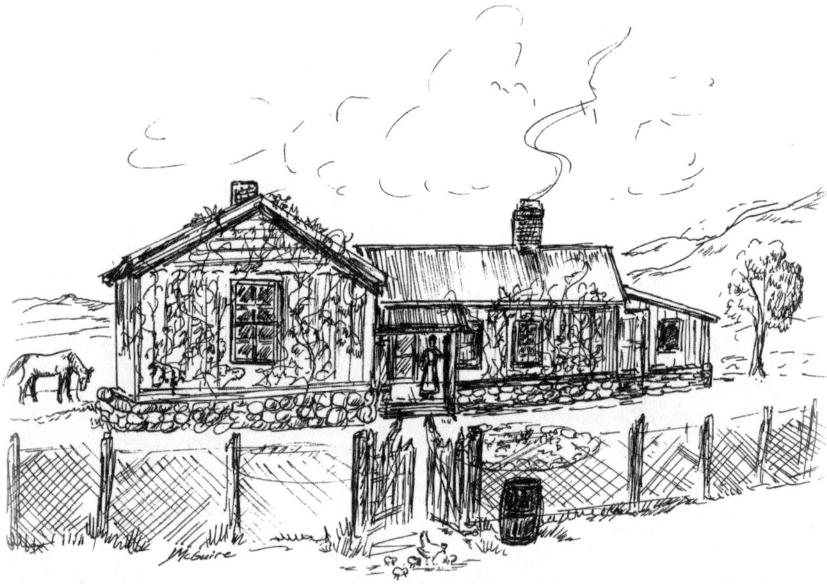

PEN & INK DRAWING OF THE LORENTZEN HOMESTEAD CABIN
BY YVONNE LORENTZEN MCGUIRE.

CHAPTER 2

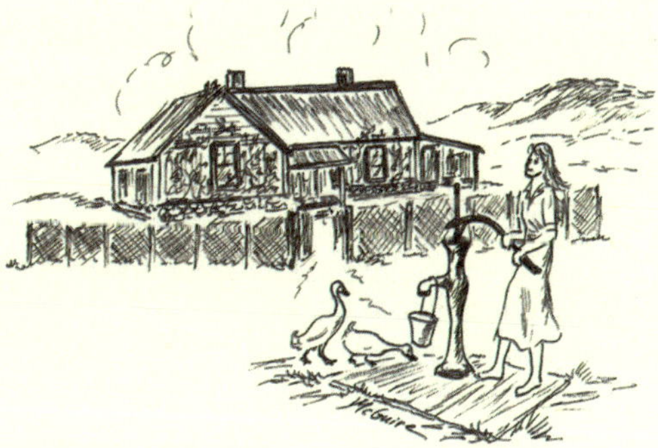

The Homestead Cabin

Growing up in this historical setting gave me a keen interest and appreciation for the old Lorentzen homestead. The cabin was built of huge hand-hewn square-sided cottonwood logs, eight to ten inches thick in both directions showing the hewn marks of the ax. They were set vertically in the ground in stockade fashion, rather than horizontally like a traditional cabin. Around the bottom of the cabin was a stone retaining wall, about three feet from the cabin walls filled with earth which gave extra strength and insulation for the walls. This dirt-filled retaining wall became an ideal place for wild wood ivy vines that flourished over the years to cover the east walls of the cabin up to the rooftop. To our sorrow, the old cabin was destroyed by fire in October 1964. In my mind's eye, I still can picture each room and the significant contents which gave me such a deep sense of my family heritage and history.

The most lasting memories are from the summer of 1952 when I was sixteen years old; I stayed in the old homestead log cabin to help my Grandma Martha who was eighty-five years old. In the springtime she had fallen, breaking her hip and was confined to a wheelchair. So I had the opportunity to become acquainted with my Grandma, as never before, and to love and appreciate her and her old home.

One of my earliest childhood memories, though, is my father taking me to visit my grandmother. We entered the fenced yard by way of a picket gate which automatically swung shut by the weight of an Indian stone hammerhead suspended from a pulley and rope. The path leading to the kitchen porch was bordered by Indian stone hammerheads. These were found and collected while tilling the fields. In my childish imagination, these fields were where Indians had camped or a battle had been fought.

On either side of the path was a flower bed of marigolds circled by stones shaded by a few small trees. Now, I wonder how my grandmother kept her flowers and trees alive during the hot dry grasshopper-infested spells of the summer. Water would have to be carried in buckets from the well and at the end of the flowering season the seeds dried and saved for the next spring planting. The influence of my grandmother's appreciation for beauty and design was passed down to my father's artistic expression with brush and paint, and to me with my artwork, home decorating and flower gardens.

Walking up the path to the kitchen porch, the busy twittering of birds could be heard in the dense shady ivy vines covering the logs at the front of the cabin. It seemed like a cool haven from the hot winds blowing across the prairie. On the left side of the porch by the door stood an old wooden ice box with brass hinges and latches. In past times, it was supplied with blocks of ice chopped from the frozen river or creek in winter, covered with straw and stored in a root cellar dug in the hillside. The insulated ice lasted way into summer.

Opening the screen door and wooden kitchen door, we stepped into a large rectangular room with white washed plaster smoothed over the log walls. A large, long wooden table with linoleum covering stood in the middle of the bare scrubbed wooden floor. On the table were a kerosene lamp, salt and pepper shakers, and a cut glass container holding teaspoons for the convenience of anyone needing a spoon during a meal.

Unnoticed to the casual eye, was a trap door under the table in the floor leading to the dirt cellar under the kitchen. To access the cellar, the table had to be moved to one side and the heavy wood door raised and propped up so someone could descend steps into the cellar. Here, potatoes and other root vegetables were stored in the cool darkness, and glass jars of canned vegetables and fruit were stored on shelves.

This reminds me of a story of my father when he was a baby. When I was a child, I noticed that the little finger on my father's left hand was misshapen on the end. The fingernail curled down over the end of his finger. While holding his hand and examining this unusual finger, I asked him what had happened to it. He told the story of how, when he was a baby, he was creeping on the kitchen floor. Someone had raised the cellar door to get something without regard of his safety. Just as he crept to the edge of the open cellar, one of his older sisters suddenly noticed he was about to fall and quickly dropped the heavy door down. In the nick of time, it saved him from falling, but the door came down on his little finger, nearly cutting the end of it off. His mother Martha quickly came to his rescue. With a strip of clean cloth, she brought the almost severed tip of his finger together and bound it tightly. This is just one example of how a pioneer woman, such as my grandmother, had to meet emergencies without a doctor and modern medical supplies. There were no Band-Aids, antiseptics, or sterilized gauze. Under her care, my father's finger grew back together and healed, but the little fingernail was permanently curled over in an abnormal way.

Situated between two doors on the north kitchen wall was a large black cast iron cook stove with ornate nickel trim around the oven door with the logo "Monarch" inscribed in the middle of the door. To the left of the oven was a door to insert wood into the firebox. Below the firebox, was a door with a compartment holding a metal pan which caught the ashes. On the top surface of the stove were four round lids to be lifted off with a special stove handle. If more direct heat was desired on the bottom of a frying pan or kettle, the lid was removed giving direct contact with the fire or hot coals below in the firebox. This, however, resulted in the bottom of the pans and sometimes the sides being blackened with smoke and carbon. If less heat was desired, the pans or kettles were moved back or to the side away from the firebox. Of course there were no gauges like modern gas and electric stoves. The cook learned from experience how much kindling or wood was needed to burn to get the desired temperature.

To the right of the cook top was a reservoir attached to the stove where a supply of water was kept that had been carried from the well out in the yard. This handy supply of water was warm or hot when the stove was being fired and was used for dish washing or hand washing. Above on the back of the stove, were two side-by-side compartments with doors known as warming ovens where food could be held and kept warm until serving time, or pans and lids could be stored there. Centered between the warming ovens was the stovepipe which ran up to enter the chimney flue. Alongside the stove, a large wooden box was filled both in winter and summer with firewood and kindling to fire up the cook stove. In the summer, the fire was kept burning only long enough to cook the breakfast oatmeal or other meals when the time came.

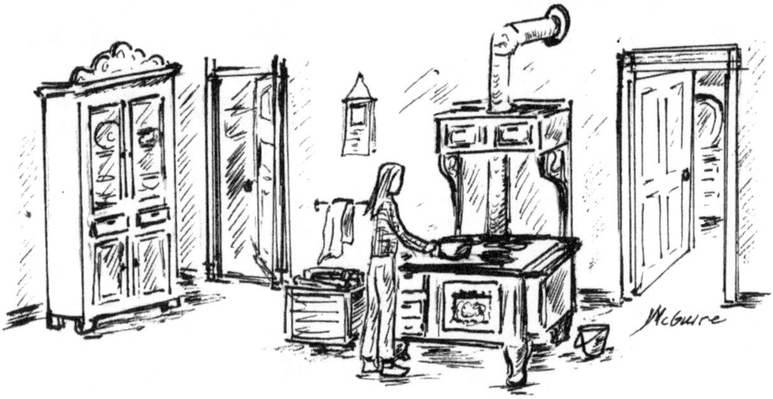

At least once a week, regardless of summer heat, the cook stove was fired up to bake bread. Usually the bread dough was mixed, worked down, and allowed to rise very early in the morning so the bread could bake in the cooler part of the day. What a delicious treat it was to eat the warm fresh slices spread with butter and clover honey! The bread flour was ground at the mill in Washburn from wheat raised on the homestead fields. My grandmother stored the flour in one-hundred pound cloth bags, supplying her household and the families of her married sons, Henry –my father– and Haldor, who lived nearby.

At the west end of the kitchen, a window unadorned by curtains provided a view of the grassy backyard and distant fields and hills beyond. Sometimes, a horse was picketed grazing in the yard so there was no need of a lawn mower. In the late afternoon or early evening as the sun was lowering in the west, an old green fabric roller shade would be pulled down to shut out the glare of the sun's last rays upon the supper table. In the evening, the westward hills were beautifully silhouetted against the matchless fire of the prairie sunset.

Underneath the window, a large wooden box with a closed lid served as a seat at the table if necessary. It held the large homemade crusty loaves of bread my grandma baked. Stored with the bread was an old Blue Willow plate upon which the delicious thick sliced bread was always served at each meal. The blue and white design on the plate was of an ancient Chinese pagoda, a temple in the form of a pyramidal tower of several stories, and a foreign looking boat sailing upon a river under an arched bridge with wild birds flying above. It held a fascination for me and seemed to be calling me to faraway places someday.

To the left of the window, a wooden corner shelf displayed the old family pendulum clock, where for perhaps 60 years or more its steady rhythmic tick-tocking and hourly melodious chiming and striking had marked the passing of time. Somehow it gave a sense of peace and comfort. Above the table on the south wall hung a large framed picture in sepia tones of several beautiful Arabian horses tossing their flowing manes and tails as they splashed through swirling ebb tide waters. Perhaps it was a lithograph or print from the work of a French artist whose similar pictures I recall from an art history course I took years later.

To the right of the west window, a china cupboard with glass doors displayed plates, cups, and a few beautiful large serving bowls with lovely hand painted roses which my grandmother treasured, saving their use for special occasions with guests. Turning them over, it was interesting to read the trademarks of the manufacturing companies in England. Beneath the glass cupboard doors were two shallow side-by-side drawers. The one on the left held black-handled knives and forks. The forks had three pronged sharp tines that were handy for spearing meat and potatoes, but required caution when taking the food into your mouth.

The right drawer held the greatest fascination for me. In it were miscellaneous articles. Of special interest, though, was the brass telescope of Grandpa Lorentz Lorentzen from his seafaring days. By adjusting the lens, you could see things miles away. Occasionally, my sister Estell and I were allowed to borrow it. Climbing the hill behind our little white house, we had a sneak peek into a ranch yard miles across the river where we might catch a glimpse of Estell's high school classmate riding his horse. In those days, if we had a "crush" on a boy, special pains were taken to not let him know.

From the vantage point of this high hill, it was exhilarating to view the great expanse of rolling prairie hills and coulees, the wooded bottomland, and the distant Missouri River to the south, with hazy square buttes miles away. A great feeling of freedom would sweep over me to lay my body against the wind with raised arms above my head, my hair blowing wildly back. Leaning into the wind, I was upheld by its driving force.

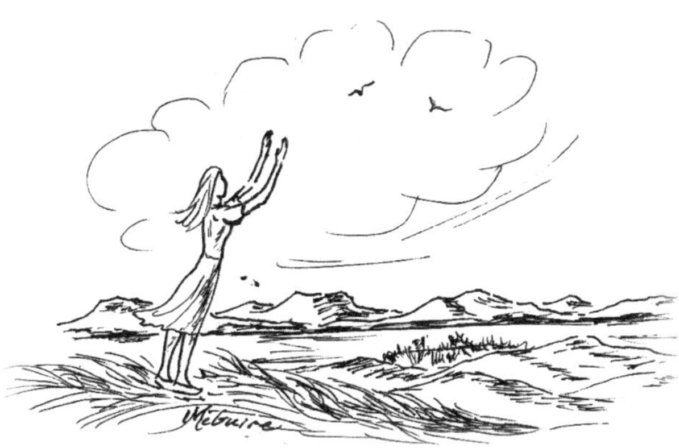

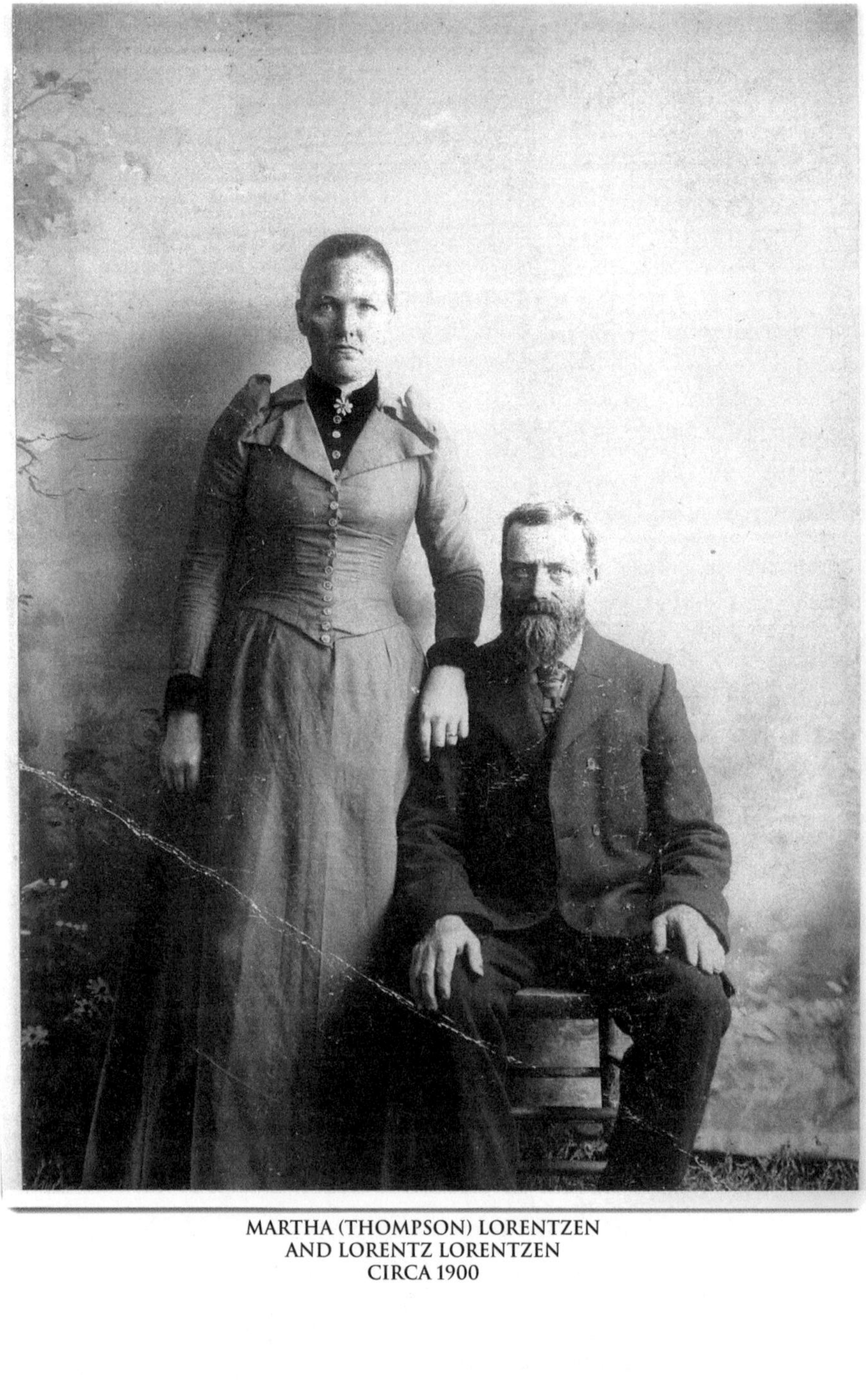

MARTHA (THOMPSON) LORENTZEN
AND LORENTZ LORENTZEN
CIRCA 1900

CHAPTER 3

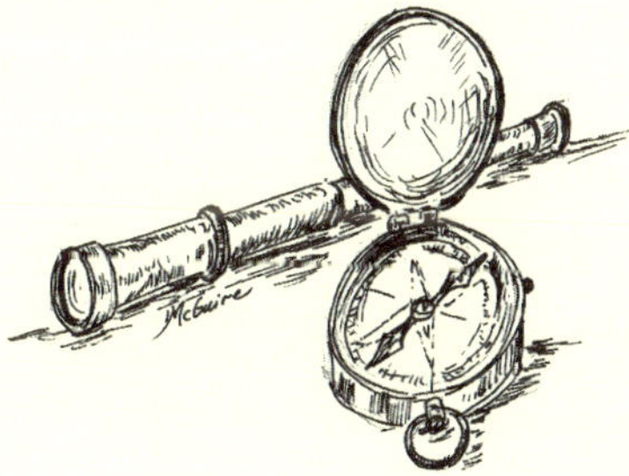

Grandfather Lorentz

The old telescope seemed to be a link to the daring adventuresome Norwegian grandfather we never had the privilege of knowing. It felt good to hold the smooth brass surface where his hands had rested. In my mind, I could see him climbing the rigging of his ship to the "crow's nest" on the tall mast to peer through this very telescope to sight land or identify the flags of an approaching vessel. Sometimes I wondered what he looked like and wished I could have known him. I felt the loss my father must have suffered, losing his father at the young age of six with very little memory of him remaining.

My father had an old studio photograph of his father Lorentz and his mother Martha taken probably in the early 1900s. Lorentz was a strong, stalwart man. My brother Norman recalled our father showing him this portrait and saying that his father Lorentz was six feet, four inches tall, weighed 250 pounds, and was called the "runt of the litter". Lorentz's height was passed on to his son Louis, to grandsons Norman and Ross Lorentzen and to great-grandson Duvon McGuire. There are great-great-grandsons who also are well over six feet tall. The photo doesn't show Lorentz's height because of the tradition of having the man seated and the woman standing, I guess, perhaps, to show off her dress. In the custom of the times, having a portrait taken was a serious matter, so people posed stiffly with a stern, sober expression. The cameraman maybe advised them not to move or smile.

Lorentz was not a farmer and tiller of the soil. He was a skilled carpenter, having worked as a shipbuilder. To support his young, growing family, he found employment in Washburn doing carpentry work and painting. John Satterlund hired him to work as a handyman about his hotel while he was away with legislative duties.

In 1903, Lorentz was hired to use his carpentry skill in the most unusual way. He built the surrounding enclosure for the gallows in Washburn for the first legal hanging in McLean County. Following this grisly event, Lorentz purchased the lumber he had used around the gallows and built part of the granary on his homestead.

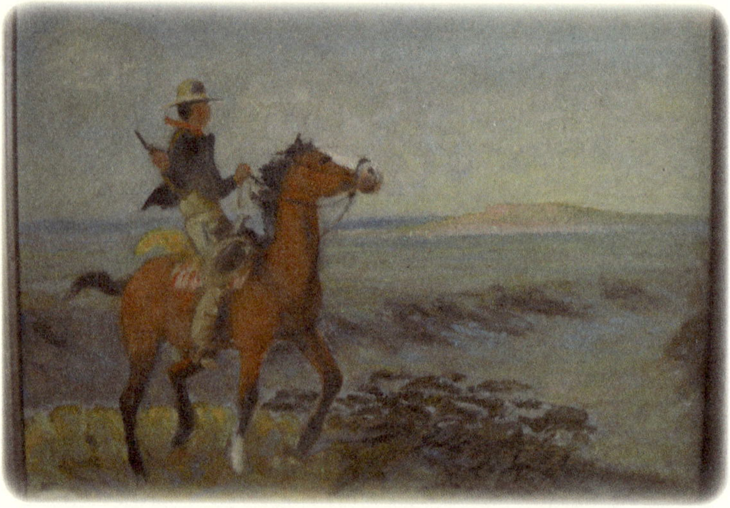

"OUTLAW ON THE RUN"
OIL PAINTING BY HENRY LORENTZEN

The story of the convict who was hanged on the gallows sounds like something out of a Wild West movie, not what one would expect to happen in the quiet farming community of Washburn. It all started when the young Bassanella brothers, Jacob and Joe, born of Italian-German immigrant parents, committed crimes back east in their New York and Pennsylvania home territory and headed West to escape arrest.

Instead of leaving their wicked ways behind and starting over with a new life, they continued their life of crime when they arrived in Grand Forks, North

Dakota. There they robbed and killed a man in a railroad boxcar. They were caught, arrested, and put in jail. While awaiting trial, they managed to escape, along with other prisoners.

The younger brother, Joe, was recaptured and sentenced to life imprisonment in the penitentiary at Bismarck. Jacob escaped. Sometime later he appeared in the Washburn vicinity under the name of James Smith. One late night, after enjoying the kind hospitality of a well-known middle-aged farmer in the area, he brutally murdered him at his bedside with a shotgun and robbed him. The stranger, James Smith, was immediately suspected of this crime. He was caught, arrested, and put in the Washburn jail, but again managed to escape while awaiting trial by removing an iron bolted hinge from his cell door and using it to dig away the mortar and stone around the window to remove the iron bars. After about three weeks of freedom, he was finally captured at Fort Yates, trying to join the Army. When he was put on trial for murder, his real identity was disclosed. James Smith was really Jacob Bassanella. On February 21, 1903, **The Washburn Leader** announced in big headlines:

> ***HANGED! Jacob Bassanella pays the penalty on the Gallows For his crime of Murder. The crime for which He Paid the Penalty Was A Most Cowardly and brutal one.***

The Washburn Leader gave details of the condemned man's walk to the gallows and of his hanging which took place within an enclosed structure next to the jail. The prisoner, attired in a black robe, was asked if he had anything to say before they pulled the black hood over his head. He replied, "Young men, don't follow in my footsteps." At seven minutes after four in the morning, by the bright light of the moon and lighted lanterns casting dark and grim shadows, the criminal life of Jacob Bassanella came to an end.

The story of the younger Bassanella brother, Joe, however would not be finished until five years later when the Washburn community would once again be involved in the most sensational manhunt in that part of the country.

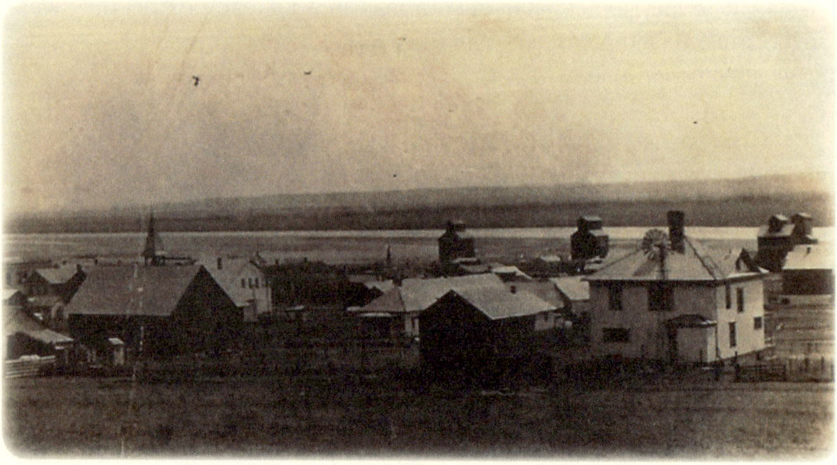

WASHBURN, NORTH DAKOTA IN EARLY 1900'S

My father said the town of Washburn, situated on the bank of the Missouri River, had a bit of atmosphere like Mark Twain's ***Tom Sawyer and Huckleberry Finn*** stories in the days of the steamboats. A ferry carried travelers back and forth across the river and other boats landed there. In my father's notes I found the following: "It happened more than once a young swimmer lost his life and too there was a heroic rescue almost every summer. Among the heroes talked about for years was Captain Leach's Newfoundland dog who plunged into the Missouri to bring to shore a young fellow who had tumbled overboard."

Lorentz probably felt more at home near the Missouri River. He was an adventuresome man who had grown up with the high, rugged mountains and fjords of Norway and had sailed the high seas for years. On the banks of the Missouri, he probably felt less like a "fish out of water" on the North Dakota prairie. He must have missed the sea with nothing to view but miles of prairie grass dipping and waving in the wind like the ocean waves. My father used to draw my attention to the flowing motion of a golden wheat field or a blue flax field in the wind like the tide rolling out. The songwriter Katharine Lee Bates, in her song *America the Beautiful*, wrote: *"O beautiful for spacious skies for amber waves of grain..."*

My father Henry quoted the following poem which expresses the deep longing his father Lorentz must have felt to once again be aboard ship sailing out to sea.

Sea Fever

I must go down to the sea again, to the lonely sea and sky,
And all I ask is a tall ship and a star to steer her by,
And the wheel's kick and the wind's song and the white sail' shaking,
and a gray mist on the sea's face and a gray dawn breaking.

I must go down to the seas again, for the call of the running tide,
Is a wild call and a clear call that may not be denied;
And all I ask is a windy day with the white clouds flying,
And the flung spray and the blown spume, and the seagulls crying.
I must go down to the seas again to the vagrant gypsy life,

To the gull's way and the whale's way, where the wind's like a whetted knife;
And all I ask is a merry yarn from a laughing fellow rover,
And a quiet sleep and a sweet dream when the long trick's over.

~ John Masefield

I wish when I was a child I had asked my father questions about his childhood and more about his father Lorentz. He did tell me he was six years old when his father died. He pointed out the location along the road to Washburn where his father had been found.

As a child, my world about me on our prairie farm was so small. I didn't grasp the enormity of the outside world and the great daring adventures of my ancestors who braved stormy seas to leave the homeland and dear ones behind to come to a strange land, to learn a new language and face the hardships of making a home on the harsh windswept prairie of North Dakota.

It was on Christmas Day in 1992 that my husband Byron and I visited my father while he was hospitalized at Bismarck. At the age of 92 he told several interesting stories that day and I jotted down notes in a little black notebook I carried. Recently I came across this notebook which reveals some early memories he had.

I asked my father how his family celebrated Christmas when he was a boy. He said his father Lorentz's sisters and their families – Elizabeth (Lisa) Knudtson and Emma Anderson – who had immigrated from Norway and lived nearby, would come for supper. They ate wonderful food. The specialty was fruit soup made with canned chokecherry juice and oatmeal with a little sugar and salt. Lefse, a special Norwegian flatbread, or thin potato cake, baked on top of the wood burning cast iron stove, was a special treat. There were delicious slices of meat from big pork or beef roasts. There were also the best doughnuts.

I asked if they received gifts. He said there would be one little toy for each child. When his father was living he received a little Noah's ark about ten inches long. It had a little cabin and roof with a number of animals. Once he got a little elephant made of cast iron about five inches tall. A little brown man, like from India, sat in a seat on the elephant's head. The head was jointed so it was slightly loose moving from side to side.

This reminds me of one of my early childhood memories. My father pretended he was an elephant to give rides to little ones. He crossed his arms in front of him with his hands locked across his forearms to make an extended square seat. He crouched down, lowering his arms so the child could sit down on his arms. Raising his arms up to about chest height, he slowly swayed from side to side as he walked around the living room like an elephant. I've never seen anyone else do this. I'm wondering if he learned this from his father. Lorentz had been a world traveler and probably had seen riders atop elephants. In Cousin Kjell Rosenberg's "The Lorentzen Saga" he tells how Lorentz's mother Ragnhild accompanied his father Captain Emanuel on a voyage to London where they visited a zoo. Ragnhild later laughingly described to her grandchildren how the big hippopotamus opened its mouth wide like a huge barn door.

On the day of November 9, 1906 the Lorentzen family had enjoyed a happy time together. Lorentz had been romping and playing with his children. Perhaps he had been giving them rides like he was an elephant. Then he set out with his team of horses to drive into Washburn to learn the election results. North Dakotans were interested in politics and were proud of Theodore "Teddy" Roosevelt, who was presently serving as 26th President of the United States. He had owned and operated cattle ranches near Medora in the Badlands of western North Dakota.

Sadly, Lorentz never arrived to hear the election results. He was found by a passing traveler on the Stone Hill about three miles west of Washburn along the Missouri River where his team of horses had stopped with their master, still clutching the reins, slumped over with a heart attack or stroke. With no snap of the reins or command of his voice, they stood with their heads down waiting for him to urge them forward. Within three days, he died. What a tragedy and shock it must have been for his wife Martha and their eight children: Edna, Estella, Hilda, Emanuel, Louis, Henry, Haldor, and Osborne – from 20-year-old Edna down to 17-month-old Osborne – to learn that he was dead at the young age of 56.

Editor Joseph Henry Taylor of **The Washburn Leader** newspaper reported Lorentzen's death with the following:

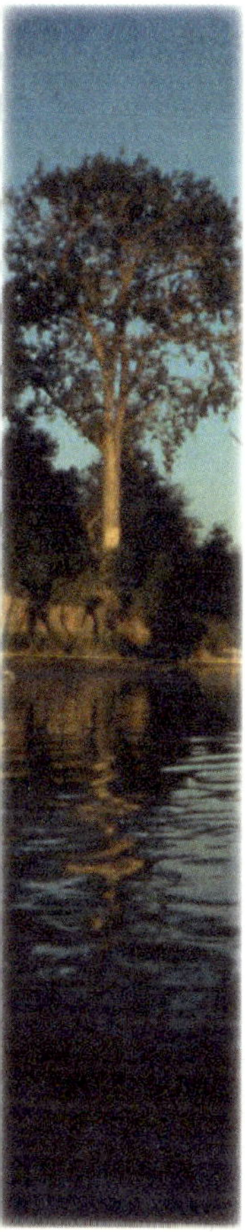

DEATH OF A PIONEER.

DIED–Last Saturday morning of paralysis. Lorentz Lorentzen, aged 56.

The deceased came to Washburn in 1886, and in 1890 he moved to Seattle, Washington. He returned to Washburn in 1892 and secured a homestead about three miles west of Washburn, where he resided continuously up to his death.

Mr. Lorentzen was born in Norway and his early life was spent on the seas and rose to the command of a ship. His papers he carefully preserved and among them was his captain's commission. He was one of the sturdy sons of Norway and by his honesty and square dealings had made for himself a name that was worth more than all the wealth of the world. All with whom he came in contact with were his friends, and they were many.

In 1884 he was married to Miss Martha H. Thompson. The funeral services were held Tuesday afternoon from the late residence, the remains being laid to rest in Riverview cemetery, followed to the last resting place by a large number of friends and relatives of the deceased.

The relatives have the sympathy of all in this their dark hour of sorrow, the loss of husband, father, brother.

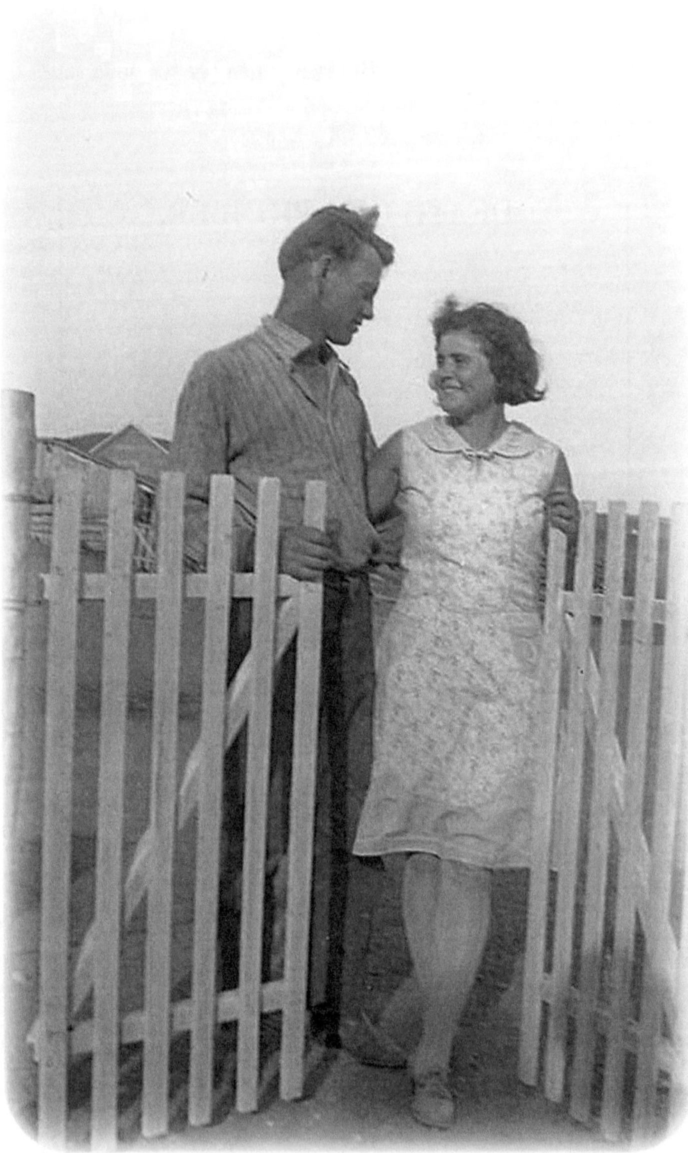

HENRY LORENTZEN AND GRACE BARLOW
BY THE HOMESTEAD YARD GATE - 1930

CHAPTER 4

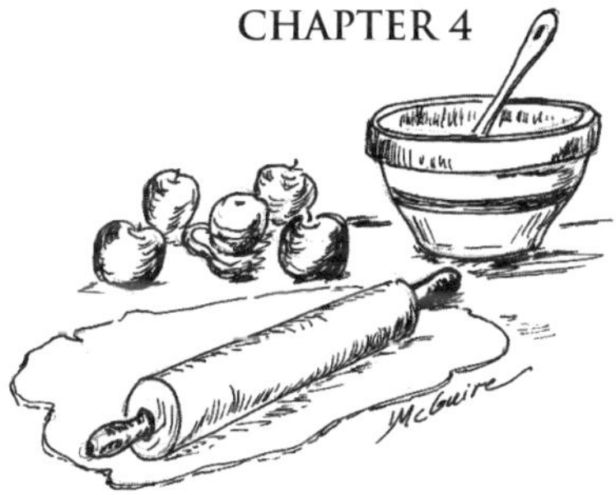

The Kitchen Gathering Room & Visitors

As I recall the old homestead cabin, its rooms and old furnishings are so intertwined with the memories of my family who lived there, and their life stories. Looking around the kitchen, we are drawn to the pantry door on the north wall between the china cupboard and the stove. The pantry was a narrow room with a small window at the end of it facing north.

In picturing the pantry, I am reminded of a little romantic story that was told about my father and mother, Henry and Grace, while they were courting. My father Henry, born in 1900, was thirty-one years old at the time. From early pictures of him, he was young and handsome with clear blue eyes and thick, light brown hair. He was a man of fine character with high moral values, and because of isolation on the homestead farm, he had little experience dating young women and girls. My mother, Grace Barlow, was a young girl of eighteen with a wealth of naturally wavy, dark brown hair and gray-green eyes. From early pictures of her and my memory she was a charming, healthy-looking, outdoor-type girl who liked to ride horseback. Though raised in town, she loved country life. Having received Christ as her personal Savior at the age of sixteen at the Asbury Camp in Washburn, she too had high moral standards and saved her kisses for the one and only man she would love and marry. She, therefore, had the ambition to marry a fine Christian rancher. Years later, she would tell her children, grandchildren, and great-grandchildren what were her criteria for a good husband. In her own words she said, "He must not smoke, drink, swear, or chase women." She happily found that my father met all her qualifications and then some.

Before their marriage in 1931, Grace was visiting Henry out at his mother's homestead. Henry asked her to come with him up a little hill north of the house where he had planted a yellow rose bush that was in full bloom. He picked her a fragrant yellow rose and presented it to her with a tender kiss and embrace. Thinking they were having a private moment behind the house, they were surprised and embarrassed to look up and see his mother, Martha, looking out the north pantry window. Since that day, yellow roses were always my mother's favorite flower.

Having heard this story as a child growing up, yellow roses were special to me as well. They became more special and significant to me, though, when the yellow rose became a symbol of love and courtship between my husband Byron and me. Without knowing the significance of yellow roses, Byron – when we were dating – had a yellow rose corsage with a black bow pinned to the visor on the passenger side of the yellow and black two-tone 1956 Chevrolet car he was driving. It did make an impression! Ever since, Byron gave yellow roses to me for special occasions.

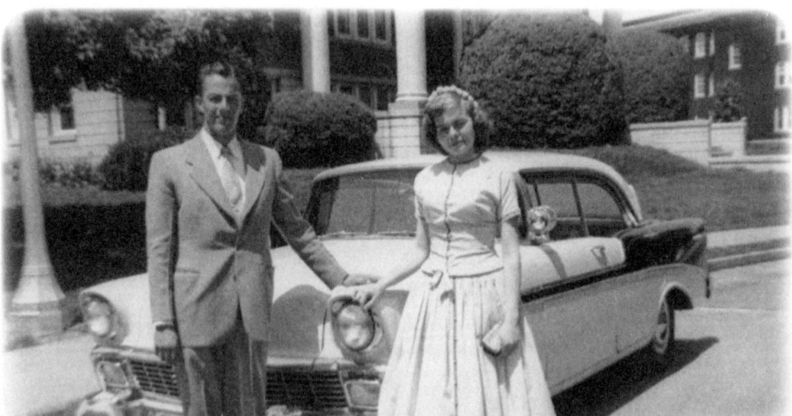

My recalling the north pantry window took us down memory lane, but we will return back to the pantry. The pantry had shelves to the ceiling where

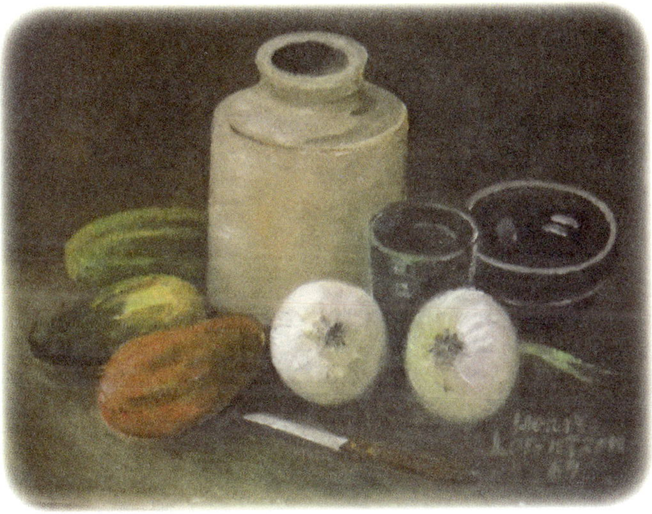

STILL LIFE OIL PAINTING BY HENRY LORENTZEN - 1969

many interesting things were displayed, such as containers of flour, sugar, salt, spices, and other supplies. Large round tins held the delicious thick sugar cookies or ginger snaps Grandma often made and served to field hands or guests for a mid-afternoon lunch. An assortment of large mixing bowls and other crockery filled the shelves. Shallow pans held skim milk to be heated slowly on the stove to make cottage cheese. Rich cream rose to the top of the containers of whole milk and was skimmed off to be churned into butter. The dish pan and other utensils hung from nails. A curiosity on the shelf was an old, dried, hardened orange decorated with cloves pressed into the rind that still smelled spicy. Perhaps it was a Christmas gift received long ago when oranges were a rare treat.

A basket of freshly-laid brown eggs sat on the pantry shelf collected each day from the hen house. Collecting eggs from the hens was one of my summer chores which caused me some anxiety and fright. A row of wooden boxes partially filled with straw was on the wall of the hen house. Here the hens laid their daily eggs. Occasionally, a hen would feel motherly or domestic, wanting to brood or sit on eggs to hatch out a family of baby chicks. We called them "cluck" hens as they made clucking sounds, like a mother hen makes when calling her chicks to her. I was to gather the eggs from these hens. When I tried to slip my hand under them to steal their eggs, I would be severely pecked. Returning unsuccessfully to the house without the eggs, my grandmother explained

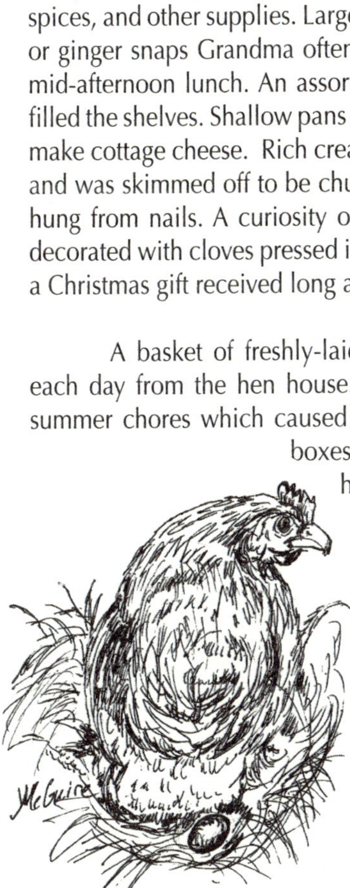

how to grab them by the back of the neck with one hand very quickly from behind and with the other hand reach under them and get the eggs while holding their head. I finally learned to do this, but felt sorry for the poor hens who wanted a family of their own.

Of most interest to me in the pantry was a perfectly constructed, made-to-scale model sailing ship of **The Noah** complete with masts, sails, and rigging, and a wooden rowboat about two feet long that were kept on the top shelf. Both were made by my Grandpa Lorentz. His father, my great-grandfather Emanuel, was captain of **The Noah**, on which they had sailed together to America. My father Henry fondly handled these cherished keepsakes when he took them down to show us children and to tell us what he remembered about his father.

We weren't allowed to play with the model ship and rowboat, though we were tempted to set them adrift in the Buffalo Paunch Creek to test them out. If we had, I feel certain we would have lost them in the swirling current that would have carried them under "Grandma's Bridge" that spanned the creek banks on the well-traveled dirt road passing by. All the people who traveled over the bridge referred to it as "Grandma's Bridge", though she wasn't their grandma, because she was well known as Grandma Lorentzen to everyone.

The summer I worked for Grandma Martha, she would sit in her wheelchair by the kitchen table and demonstrate for me how to punch down the bread dough, or how to roll out pie crusts. If I was too timidly kneading the bread dough, she would get her hands on the dough and vigorously punch it down. No doubt this gave her satisfaction to be still involved in bread making. As the ingredients for recipes were needed she taught me to bring out those things from the pantry and to return them immediately to their exact place on the shelf, so there were never accumulated items cluttering up the table. Baking utensils and bowls were washed immediately so there never was a stack-up of dirty dishes waiting to be washed at the next meal.

When cleaning off the crumbs from the table top, my grandmother taught me to catch them in my hand, and then to throw them out in the front yard where a hungry bird or creature could find something to eat. Grandma had learned to be frugal in feeding her own large family and not to be wasteful of food, so there was enough to go around to all, including guests or travelers who happened to stop on their journey to or from town. In her isolated home, she enjoyed talking with travelers who brought news of the outside world. Her excellent cooking and generosity became known far and wide.

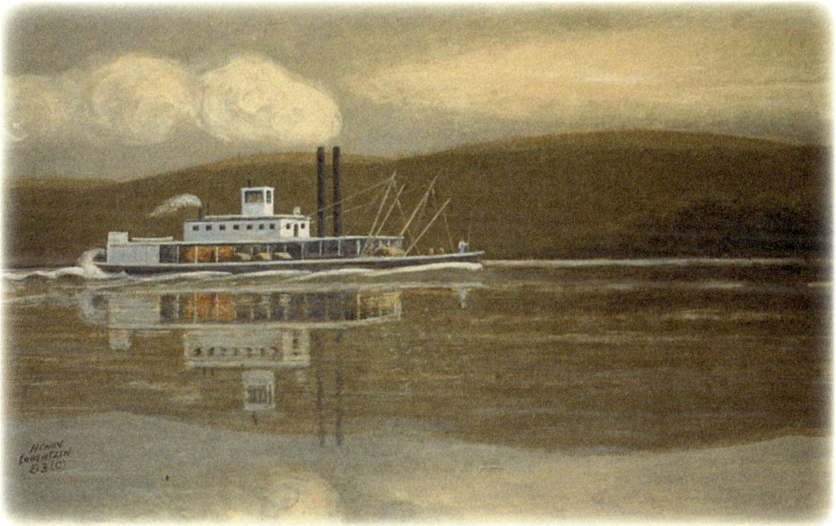

"THE FAR WEST" PILOTED BY CAPTAIN GRANT MARSH
OIL PAINTING BY HENRY LORENTZEN, 1983

A distinguished visitor in the Lorentzen home was Joseph Henry Taylor who lived in the Washburn area and was well known as a frontiersman, newspaperman, historian and author of books about frontier and Indian life. Another one of my grandmother's noted guests was Captain Grant Marsh. In 1876, Captain Marsh piloted a steamboat, *"The Far West"*, nearly a thousand miles at record speed down the Little Bighorn River, the Yellowstone, and the treacherous Missouri River steering clear of snags and sandbars to arrive at Fort Lincoln at Bismarck bearing one wounded army horse, Comanche, the only living survivor of the Custer Battle, and fifty-two critically wounded soldiers from Major Reno's command.

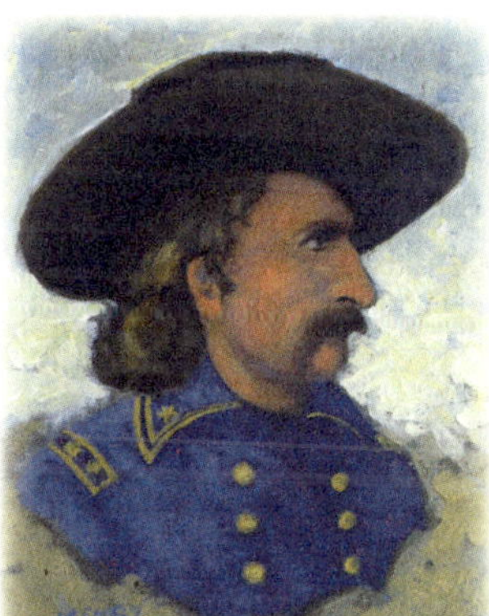

"GENERAL CUSTER" - OIL PAINTING
BY HENRY LORENTZEN

General George A. Custer over-confidently led his 7th Cavalry into battle against the Sioux Indians in the Battle of the Little Bighorn in Montana, later known as the Custer Massacre, with him and all 210 under his command killed. In his past Indian encounters, Custer had experienced fairly easy victories. Disregarding warnings from his Crow Indian scouts and unwisely separating his regiments, against the better judgment of the leaders under him, he went forward not prepared for the nearly 10,000 warriors under the leadership of Crazy Horse and Sitting Bull who lay in wait for him.

The dirt road running west of Washburn followed closely along the banks of the Missouri River and the wooded bottomland. About three miles west of town the road passed by the Lorentzen homestead. Crossing over the wooden plank bridge that spanned the Buffalo Paunch Creek the clip-clop of horses' hooves, the clatter of buggy wheels, or the bump and rumble of a lumber wagon could be heard.

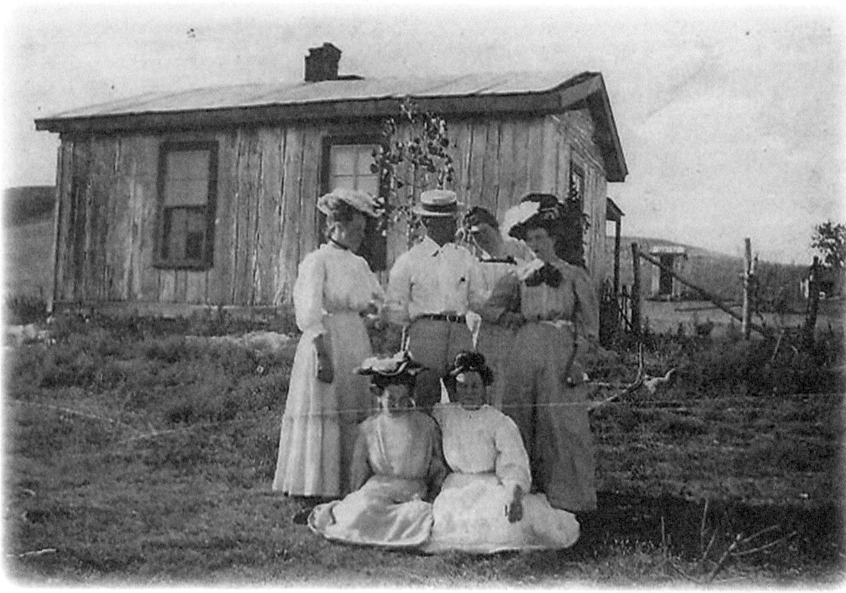

VISITORS AT THE LORENTZEN HOMESTEAD

Travelers were not frequent on the road, but when they passed by they aroused some curiosity about who they were and where they were going. More often they were friendly neighbors going to or from town. They were recognized by the kind of rig and the team of horses they were driving. A lone rider could be recognized by his stature and the color of his horse. Sometimes these folks turned in to the homestead yard for a friendly visit with the Lorentzen family, where they were welcomed into the kitchen of their log home for a bite of lunch and a cup of coffee.

On a summer day in the early 1900's, a most surprising, unbelievable cavalcade was seen passing the Lorentzen homestead on the dusty road. A circus parade with rumbling big wagons pulled by teams of horses and elephants slowly plodding along were on their way to performances up north at Underwood and beyond. The children must have run excitedly into the house to tell their mother Martha. Their sister Hilda quickly grabbed her camera and captured this memorable sight of elephants with the homestead buildings in the background.

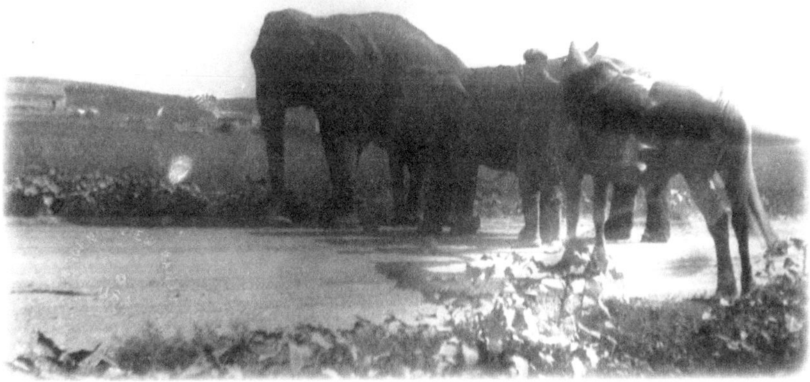

CIRCUS PARADE PASSING BY THE LORENTZEN HOMESTEAD

With the hint of coming spring in the air, the Lorentzen brothers were enjoying playing in their homestead yard on a March day in 1908. Lingering snow banks were ideal for making snowballs, a fort or sliding down the hills on their home-made wooden sleds. Suddenly, the rapid hoof beats of a running horse on the road caught the boys' attention. They looked up to see a strange man on a white horse galloping westward. There was something mysterious and sinister about him. What could be his hurry? Even more intriguing, the boys later saw two men with a team and buckboard rapidly travelling west like they may be pursuing the horseman. As the afternoon wore on, they were shocked to see the two men slowly returning east toward Washburn. The legs of a man dangled off the end of the buckboard. My father, Henry, who was eight at the time witnessed these happenings and years later told his children and grandchildren about it. The rest of the story unfolds from an old edition of **The Washburn Leader**, researched by my great-niece, Amanda Lorentzen, including additional details learned and told by my father.

On March 20, 1908 Fred Pfister was on his way to Washburn with a load of coal from the mine west of Washburn when he met a stranger riding a white horse who stopped to inquire about the river road and location of crossings on the Missouri River. The rider then rode ahead west. Pfister eyed the man and thought the stranger looked suspicious. After unloading his coal in town, he learned of an escaped convict and informed Sheriff Beck of his encounter.

The sheriff told Pfister that the Washburn community had been alerted of the escape of the criminal Joe Bassanella from the Bismarck penitentiary. He was the younger brother of Jacob Bassanella who was hung on the gallows in Washburn five years earlier in 1903. Joe and another prisoner, both sentenced to life, escaped from the penitentiary through a tunnel 44 feet in length that they dug with a piece of iron and a chisel beneath the wood floor of a carpenter shop where the prisoners worked. The other prisoner named Wollen was captured about seventeen miles west of Mandan. Bassanella was still on the loose. From reports of a home robbed of a pistol and ammunition, and a horse stolen at another location, it was determined that the escaped convict was moving north. Washburn Sherriff Beck was notified to be on the lookout. Could he be headed to Washburn to avenge the hanging of his brother Jacob by the now-retired Sheriff Ole Gradin?

The sheriff deputized Pfister, and immediately they set out with a team of horses and a light wagon in pursuit. About ten miles west they learned that the stranger had been seen passing by a farm and he had eaten lunch at another farm. Continuing west, they saw a man on a white horse ahead. As they drew closer, the man urged his horse to a faster gait, leading the pursuers over plowed fields and rougher country headed for the woods. By this time the sheriff and Pfister were certain the man was Bassanella, who now dismounted and on foot headed for the timber. The pursuers abandoned their team and for the first time shot at the fleeing criminal, who did not heed their commands to stop and surrender. The convict took refuge in a thicket in a coulee.

Years later when my father was a man, he became personally acquainted with Fred Pfister, who told him exactly how the shootout took place and pointed out the spot in the coulee where Bassanella hid. Sheriff Beck and Pfister had lost sight of Bassanella's whereabouts until Pfister saw a slide mark in the snow where Bassanella had slid down into a washout hidden in the snow. They were within a hundred yards from him when Bassanella opened fire at them with his stolen pistol. Fred said he felt the bullets hitting his heavy sheepskin-lined overcoat. It was then that Sheriff Beck yelled, "Let him have it!" They both began to fire at Bassanella, who was well hidden in the washout, but occasionally showed his head. Fred Pfister told my father that he carefully raised his 30-30 rifle, held it steady, and pulled the trigger. Thus ended the career of a cold-blooded murderer and brought to end the most sensational man hunt in that part of the country.

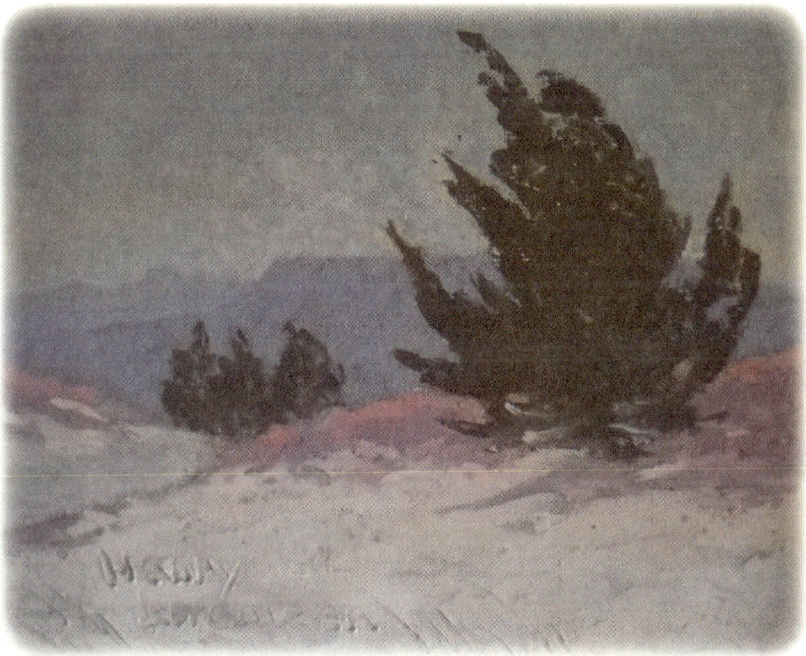

"WINTER LANDSCAPE"
OIL PAINTING BY HENRY LORENTZEN

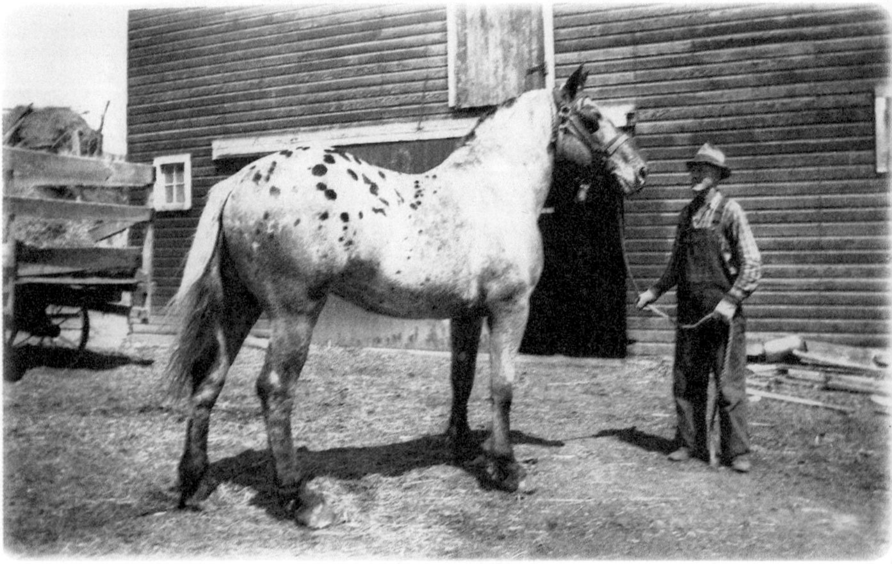

UNCLE EMANUEL
WITH DRAFT HORSE

CHAPTER 5

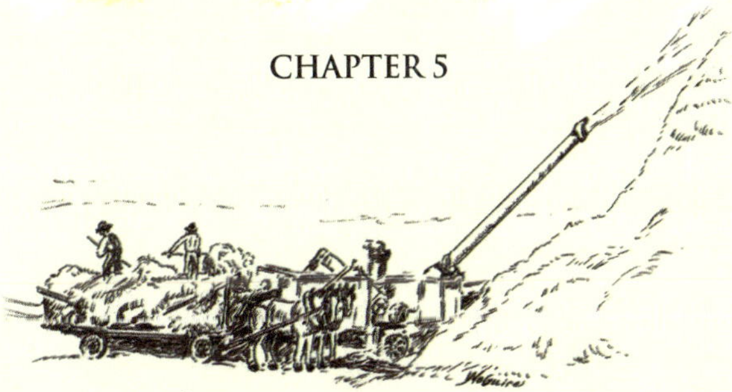

Uncle Emanuel

To the right of the cook stove on the northeast end of the kitchen was a door leading to Uncle Emanuel's room. It was a small room large enough for a bed, a dresser, and a window facing the east. It always seemed shadowy and dark with ivy vines partly over the window nearly shutting out the daylight. There were pegs or hooks for clothes on the wall. Nothing much is known about this private room, because it was considered off-limits to children. Uncle Emanuel, born in the year 1895 was the oldest son who took a load of responsibility upon his young shoulders following the death of his father. He served as a soldier in World War I in France and saw action in the Argonne Forest and Thiecourt sectors. Memorabilia from France and some of his World War I uniforms hung behind the door in his room. Uncle Emanuel was a hard-working man who rose early at daybreak to work in the fields or to care for the animals, and went to bed when the day's labors were brought to a close by nightfall.

Uncle Emanuel was a wonderful handler of horse teams, and had a beautiful pair of matched golden Palomino draft horses perhaps of mixed Belgian or Clydesdale breeding. They were huge, heavily muscled, and had dark shiny coats with snowy white manes and tails. Long hair hung at their fetlocks above their huge hooves. They were very gentle and well trained and responded obediently to his slightest command. He used them for all kinds of farm work: mowing, raking, stacking hay, and hauling heavy loads. My brother Ross recalls how the school bus on which he was riding was stuck in deep mud, not far from what was known as the "Lorentzen Hill," west of the Lorentzen home place. The bus driver had no solution to his dilemma, until Ross suggested his Uncle Emanuel lived nearby and had a team of horses that could pull the bus out, which he did better than a wrecker probably could have.

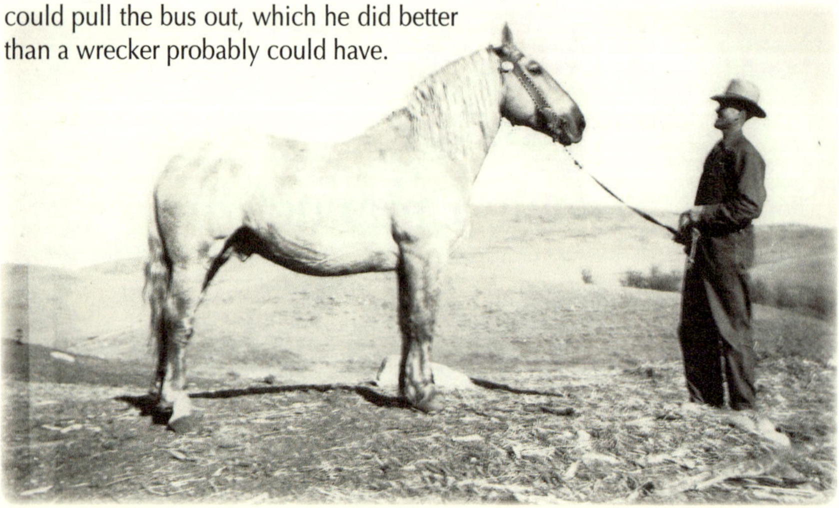

UNCLE EMANUEL WITH DRAFT HORSE

I remember Uncle Emanuel as a kind man of medium height and slight build. Usually attired in work bib overalls, he worked tirelessly. He did not take time out for long conversations or storytelling. Emanuel had a quiet sense of humor and a suppressed laugh, almost like he was trying to hold it in while his shoulders would shake. My brother Norman recalled how he and Uncle Emanuel could have a conversation, and days later, Uncle Emanuel would take up talking where they left off as if no time had passed. Uncle Emanuel was named after his grandfather, Captain Emanuel Lorentzen, so at times he was called "Captain". At the table, he sat in a chair with arms on it known as a captain's chair.

Uncle Emanuel took time out from his many summer duties to pick wild plums, chokecherries, and Juneberries in the coulees to bring home for his mother to can into sauce or make jelly or pies. While picking chokecherries, he would eat handfuls of them, carefully separating the small, dark fruit from the hard seed with his teeth and tongue and spitting out the seeds. When he arrived in the kitchen proudly carrying the fruits of his labors, it was laughable to see that the chokecherries had stained his teeth a dark brown, making him look toothless.

One hot summer day, I was cleaning the old cast iron "Monarch" cookstove. The fire in it was allowed to go out and the stove had cooled.

Grandma showed me how to put some kerosene in a tin can, and with a rag, polish the stove and all the nickel chrome. I was working on this when Uncle Emanuel came in with his empty glass gallon jug to fill with water from the reservoir before taking it out with him to do field work. Usually a tin can sat by the reservoir to use as a dipper for water. Unbeknownst to me, he picked up my kerosene can, dipped it into the reservoir and filled his jug. He then tipped the jug up to take a big swig of water and immediately lowered the jug sputtering, coughing, and uttering words that are unprintable. Probably his worst fault was swearing, if there was a calamity or something bad had happened. Grandma sat in her wheelchair nearby and in a sorrowful voice was softly saying "Uff-da, Uff-da, Uff-da!" In Norwegian, I'm not sure exactly what it means, but it seems to express a multitude of feelings or emotions. I'm sure it grieved her to hear her son's bad language, and to also know that the water jug as well as the reservoir were contaminated by kerosene. Humorously, the Norwegian expression, "Uff-da," is uttered today by Grandma's descendants under unusual circumstances.

Because Uncle Emanuel devoted his entire life to working on the homestead, he probably never took the time to socialize or make an acquaintance with a woman who would be willing to share the hardships of farm life and the home of his widowed mother. He remained single, managing the homestead farm, until his death from lung failure in November 1959. During World War I, Uncle Emanuel's lungs had been burned with mustard gas in the Argonne Forest. Ever since, cold air affected his lungs.

To my knowledge, Uncle Emanuel did not talk about the horrific experiences in World War I and the effects of the enemy's poisonous gas upon him. Perhaps because it had happened so long ago in 1918, he no longer thought about it. He was one of the many unsung heroes who, upon returning home, quietly worked to rebuild their life. He faithfully toiled on the homestead his parents had begun and over the years bought more acreage adjoining it. Having no wife and children of his own, he valued and appreciated the offspring of his brothers and his sisters.

At the time of Uncle Emanuel's death, I was living in Indiana so I missed his last days and his funeral. My mother told the news in a letter. My brother Ross, who had been enrolled with a basketball scholarship at LeTourneau Technical Institute in Longview, Texas, came home in time to dig the grave for Uncle Emanuel. While digging in the hard frozen ground and then encountering a huge rock which he lifted out by hand, he suffered an attack of appendicitis and was taken to a Bismarck hospital for immediate surgery. He missed the funeral. After recovery, he did not return to Texas.

In the winter of 1954-1955, my folks, with my brother Ross, moved to

Ruso, ND to take care of a friend's farm during their prolonged absence. My brother Norman stayed in the old log home with Grandma Lorentzen, Uncle Louie and Uncle Emanuel to help them and attend the public school at Washburn. Norman shared Uncle Emanuel's little bedroom with him and recalls how cold it was in the winter with inch-thick frost on the inside log wall near the window. Norman, whose middle name is Emanuel, felt a special closeness to his uncle, and recently said he wished he had given Uncle Emanuel a hug when he told him goodbye before he left to join the Navy in January 1959, not knowing it was his last time to see him alive.

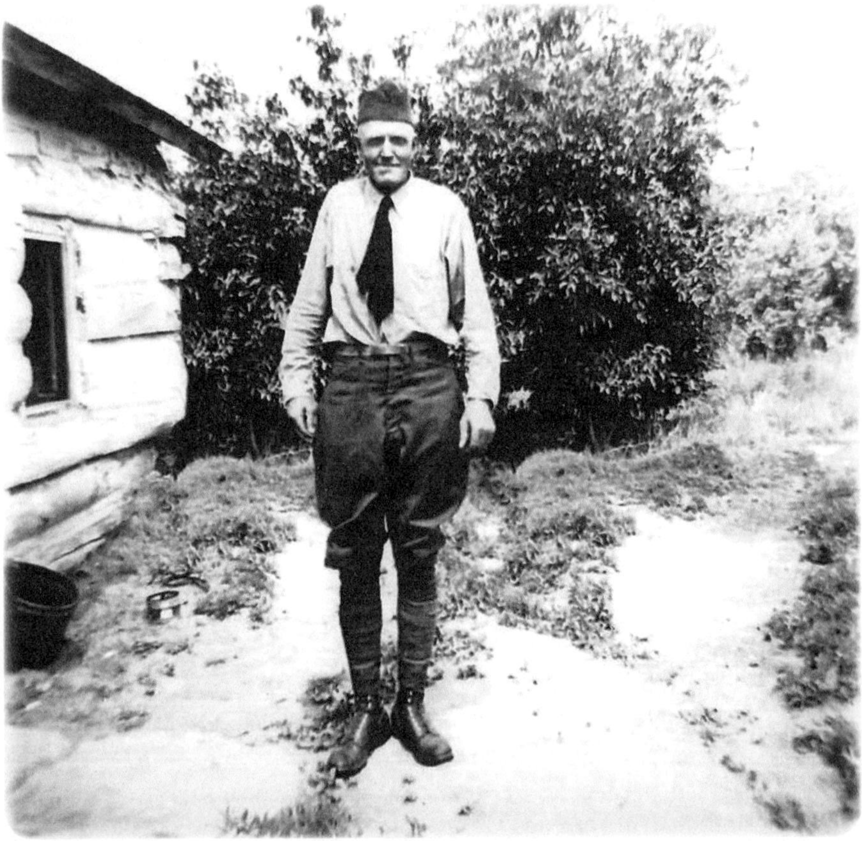

UNCLE EMANUEL
IN WORLD WAR I UNIFORM

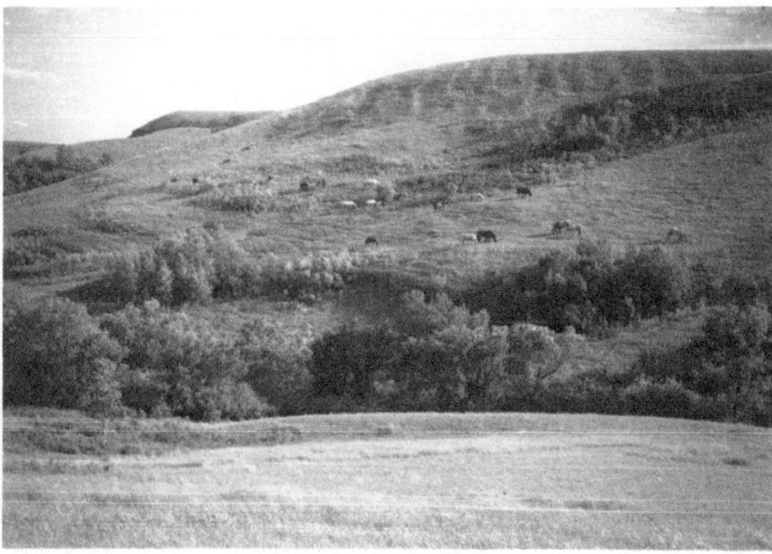

HORSES GRAZING ON THE HILLS
OF BUFFALO PAUNCH CREEK

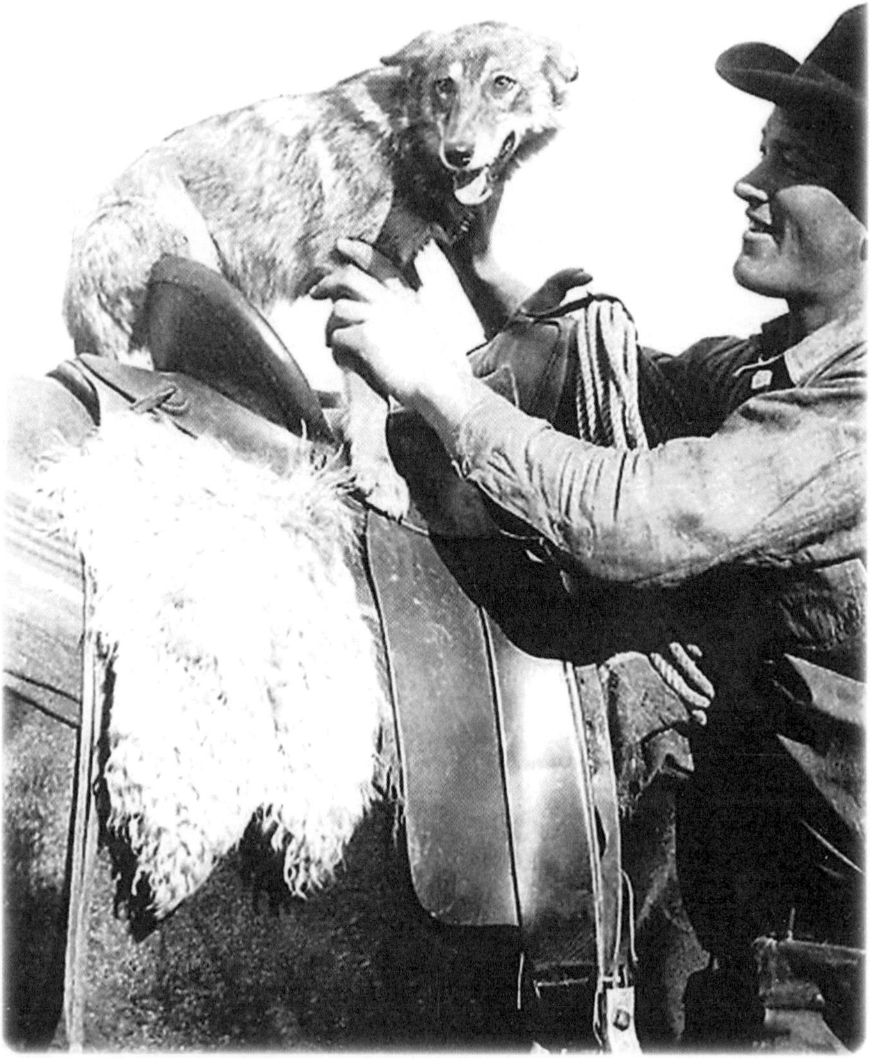

LOUIE LORENTZEN WITH PET HALF-BREED COYOTE

CHAPTER 6

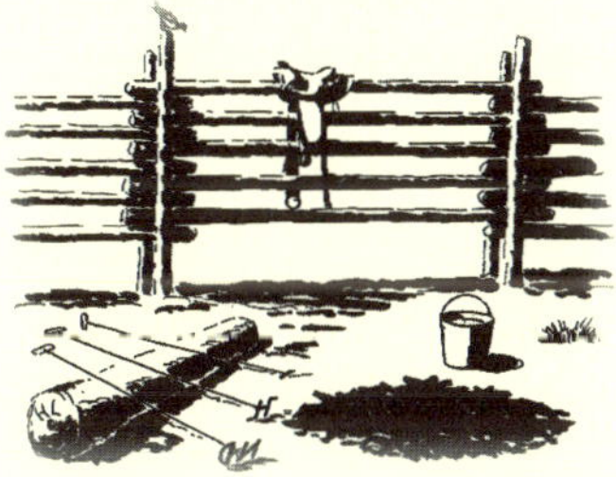

Uncle Louie

Next to Uncle Emanuel's bedroom door on the east wall, stood an old wringer washing machine with a gasoline motor attached. Wash day was a big undertaking. I recall water being carried by buckets from the farmyard well, and heated in a boiler on the stove. The heated water was then dumped into the tub of the washer, and the dirty clothes put in to be agitated with the engine driven dasher. The light-colored or white clothes and linens were washed first in the washer, and then denim overalls or dark clothes were put in last in the same water. When washed sufficiently, the clothes were guided by hand through the tightly pressed rollers of the wringer to squeeze out the water, being careful not to wind up the ends of the garment or your fingers. The clothes were then run into a tub of rinse water, where they were swished up and down by hand, and then were finally run through the wringer again to be hung outdoors on the clothesline. Needless to say people in those days did not change their clothes as frequently as people nowadays do.

Between the washing machine and the entrance door was a wash stand which held a bucket of water with a dipper, a metal wash pan, a bar of soap, and a roller towel. There was a bucket on the floor to hold used wash water. The bucket was emptied in the yard to water a tree or a flowerbed.

Behind the kitchen door in the left hand corner was an old Windsor backed chair with shortened legs that had been worn down from much use. On the wall in the corner were my Uncle Louie's angora chaps and an assortment of lariats, bridles, coats, and his western cowboy hat.

My Uncle Louis (always pronounced with the French pronunciation, Louie) was born in 1897 and also never married. He spent his lifetime working on the homestead and caring for his widowed mother, my Grandma Martha. From old black and white photos taken in the early 1920's, Uncle Louie was a handsome, tall horseman riding bucking broncos. He was a skilled hunter and excellent marksman with a gun, providing wild game for the table such as venison, quail, pheasants, and geese.

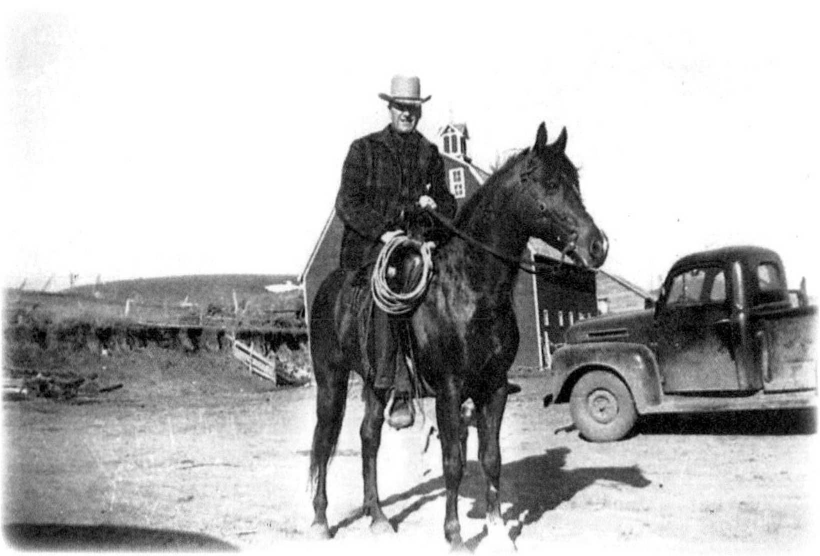

Uncle Louie was a great storyteller with a sense of humor and a hearty laugh. His witty humorous remarks or stories are recalled to this day by those who heard them. The following story I heard him tell. I'm not sure if he personally witnessed this happening, or possibly was the instigator of it.

There was a young handsome cowboy at a rodeo who had made the acquaintance of an admiring pretty young lady and was engaged in conversation with her obviously making quite an impression. A couple of the cowboy's friends enviously stood on the sidelines. Finally one of them had an ingenious idea. Not far off he spotted an Indian boy, shabbily dressed, who was about eight years old. He went over to the boy and said, "Would you like to earn some money? See that cowboy over there talking to that lady? Here is a quarter if you go over to him, pull on his coat and say, 'Come on, Dad. Let's go home'." You can imagine "the rest of the story!"

I remember Uncle Louie as a western cowboy-type man resembling the Hollywood movie star John Wayne in appearance and mannerisms. He was a kind, big-hearted man who gave special attention to his nephews and nieces. As his nephews were growing up and becoming taller, he in fun liked to compare his six-and-a-half foot height with their own height. He showed off his ability to touch the kitchen ceiling with his hand flattened against it, and he compared his arm span with the length of their arms. Occasionally he would pick us up after school to drive us home and would stop by the drugstore in town to buy us nickel ice cream cones which were a real treat for us. My brother Ross has said that Uncle Louie was kind of a grandfather figure for us children since he was older than our father, and we did not know our real grandfather because of his early death.

Uncle Louie would take out time to teach us how to use a lariat or lasso to practice roping. He was very skillful at roping cattle or wild horses in a corral. One of his roping skills was called "throwing the hoolihan", keeping the opened loop of the lariat low at his side where a wary animal would not see it, and then suddenly throwing it out with lightning speed like a striking snake to snare the unsuspecting animal. He also knew some trick roping skills and could whirl a huge round loop around his body and jump in and out of it or whirl a smaller loop horizontally in front of him and vertically at his side. He patiently taught me how to make a loop with the rope and to whirl it around my head to release it at just the right time to settle over a fence post or other object while keeping hold of the end of the rope with the other hand. This became a sort of entertainment for me to practice until I became quite skilled at judging distance and the amount of force in releasing the loop to have it settle over its intended target.

My brothers, sister, and I practiced roping the pail-fed calves in their barnyard pen when our mother wasn't looking. Sometimes we took turns with the lariat to rope our siblings as they ran past us. Our old paint cowhorse, Pocah, patiently allowed us to ride her by at a gallop while the roper on the ground tried to lasso her. It is a wonder she didn't rebel to dodge our poorly aimed loop at times.

The 4th of July was a big, exciting event for my brothers, sister and me when Uncle Louie would take us to the big Mandan rodeo across the Missouri River from Bismarck. It was thrilling to see the pretty girl trick-riders galloping around the arena performing their daring stunts and to see the wild bronc riding, calf roping, bulldogging, and bull riding with the clowns risking their lives to distract a charging bull from a fallen rider. The evening ended with a spectacular

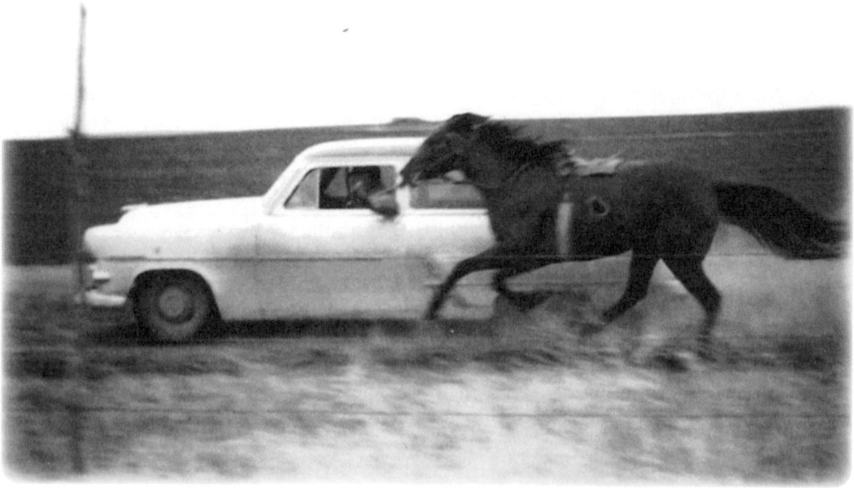

LOUIE LORENTZEN EXERCISING HIS RACEHORSE

show of fireworks. In my early teens, I had the ambition to become a cowgirl, performing in rodeos. Even though the Lord had another plan for me, my girlhood fantasy served me well.

I never would have dreamed that about thirty years later the roping skills I learned from Uncle Louie would come in handy. After serving on the mission field in Ecuador, South America, my husband Byron and I with our five children, Duvon, Josiah, Martha, Maria and Linda, returned to "Harmony Hill", our little farm in Southern Indiana. Wanting our children to enjoy horses like I had growing up in North Dakota, we bought an old Quarter Horse mare we called "Doggie" that was with foal. She gave birth to a beautiful copper-colored filly we named Penny.

When she was just a few weeks old, Penny and her mother were out in our wooded pasture. We went out to see them and were shocked to see that Penny had cut her right front leg below the knee, and it was bleeding profusely with a pulsing stream of blood spurting out. Apparently an artery was cut. We immediately caught the mare and then tried to catch the foal who was racing frantically about, causing the blood to spurt even more. A veterinarian was called and after several attempts we decided that Penny was not going to let us catch her. Byron got out a lasso he sometimes used on cattle, and attempted to rope her with no success. Finally I said, "Let me try it." I carefully built the loop and coiled the rope as Uncle Louie had taught me. To my surprise and the amazement of Byron and the children looking on, as the filly ran circling around us, I threw the loop with such precision and accuracy, it cleanly settled around her neck the first try. The filly would have bled to death if the bleeding had not been stopped. The veterinarian arrived soon to stitch and bandage her leg. I give the Lord and Uncle Louie the credit for saving the life of the filly.

The summer I worked for Grandma I was rather tall and thin with long blonde hair. My father would teasingly call me "Beanpole", but Uncle Louie called me "Vonnie" and told me I had long legs like a Thoroughbred and could run fast like one. While Uncle Emanuel's interest was in his huge draft horses, Uncle Louie's interest was in Thoroughbred race horses. He had purchased a few mares and a stallion with excellent bloodlines with some Kentucky Derby winners back in their pedigrees. My father Henry helped him in registering foals. Uncle Louie had friends involved in horseracing who helped him, so some of his horses were winning races within a two or three state area. Quite often it seemed, to Uncle Emanuel's disapproval and disgust, he was left on the farm with more than his share of the work during haying or harvest season, while Uncle Louie took off to a rodeo or the races. If Uncle Louie had had the resources and facilities of the Kentucky horse breeders, his horses could have ranked among the Kentucky Derby winners. Following in Uncle Louie's footsteps was his nephew Haldor Junior, son of Louie's brother Haldor, who became an excellent horseman, sometimes riding bucking broncs, riding Uncle Louie's race horses, and accompanying him to the races.

On the first Saturday of every May, my father would take us children over to Grandma's to gather with Uncle Louie around the battery powered radio to listen to the running of the Kentucky Derby at Churchill Downs. What a thrill it was to hear the clear call of the bugle, signaling the jockeys and horses to take their places at the starting gate, and then to hear the sweet stirring strains of Stephen Foster's "My Old Kentucky Home". Who could have guessed then that someday I would make my home in southern Indiana, just thirty-five miles north of the Ohio River from Louisville, Kentucky?

That summer at the age of sixteen I was an inexperienced cook, but with my grandma's help, I would try my best to have food prepared at mealtime. However, when my uncles came in to eat, and the food wasn't quite ready, it made me nervous to hear my Uncle Louie say, "I'm hungry as a scairt wolf!" A little trick I learned was to at least have the table set so it would appear like food was not long in coming. I don't recall my uncles wearing a wristwatch or carrying a pocket watch, but somehow they always knew to arrive for meals at the right time. Perhaps their stomachs signaled it was time to eat, but I think it was their ability to measure time by the height of the sun in the sky and the lengthening shadows across the land. The nightly ritual of Uncle Louie winding the key in the old pendulum clock in the kitchen corner before retiring for bed kept our daily routine on schedule. As my brother Ross said, "In those days each house was the center of their own time zone."

It is strange how a little remark or lesson given over fifty years ago can come to mind. For example, I can't peel a boiled egg without remembering how Uncle Louie demonstrated to me one day how it should be done. I was slowly and gingerly picking the shells from a hot boiled egg when he reached over and said, "Here, let me show you how the cowboys do it." He then took the egg in his hand, picked up his table knife and gave the blade a quick, downward slam across the middle of the egg, neatly cutting it in half. With the point of the knife, he deftly turned out the halves free of their shells in about a second. A working man didn't have time to sit around daintily picking egg shells from an egg when they needed to saddle up to round up the cattle, or get out in the hayfield before it rained. Of course, a woman making deviled eggs or sliced eggs for a salad couldn't take Uncle Louie's shortcut method. However, Uncle Louie was handy in the kitchen, cooking the morning oatmeal, frying the meat, or doing whatever needed to be done when a woman wasn't around to do it. In addition, he was a kind and considerate caregiver for his mother, helping her in and out of her wheelchair and seeing about her other personal needs.

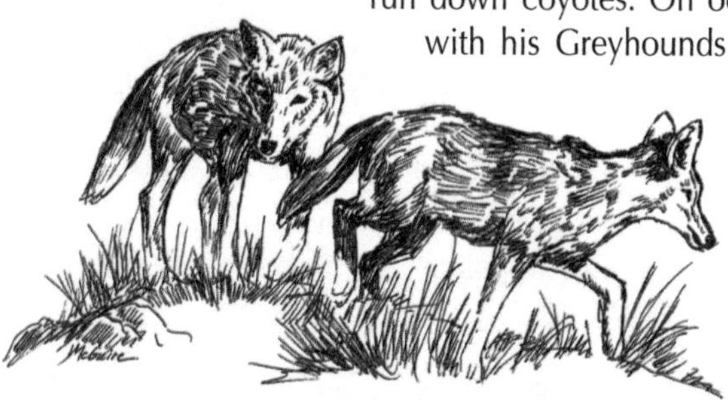

Uncle Louie raised Greyhounds and used them to run down coyotes. On occasion he would drive along with his Greyhounds in his car until he spotted a coyote and would open the door to let them out to run down the coyote. In Uncle Louie's younger years he rode horseback with his hounds. He carried his lightest weight, fastest hound always a female, with him in front of him on the saddle. She would have sharp eyes to see a coyote first from this vantage point and would also be rested up ready to run, while the bigger, stronger male hounds would be running along on the ground. When a coyote was spotted, Uncle Louie would release the female from the saddle to run it down. The hounds worked as a team to close in on the chase, cutting across corners when the coyote zigzagged to the right or left. This wasn't just for sport, but to sell the coyote pelts for needed income, and also to prevent them from eating young livestock and chickens.

In the early 1920's, Uncle Louie had a half-breed coyote. Raised by its

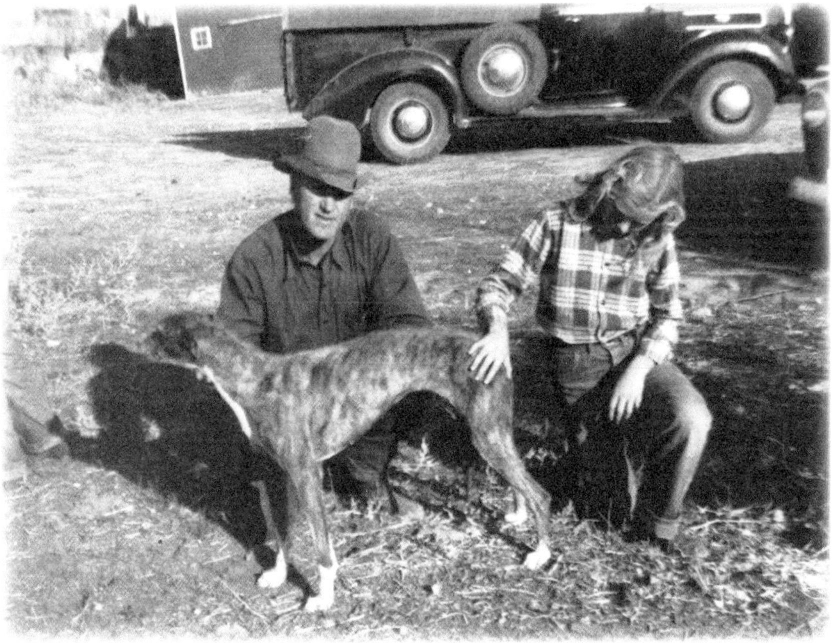

UNCLE LOUIE LORENTZEN & NIECE YVONNE WITH QUEENIE

greyhound mother, it was accepted by the rest of the greyhounds. His favorite hound, a tan brindle in color, was "Queenie". When she died of old age, one of her female offspring became the next "Queenie". Sometimes his hounds while out hunting would come across a porcupine, and would return whimpering and whining with quills stuck in their faces. Uncle Louie would bring them into the kitchen at night and by lamplight pull out the quills with pliers.

From the kitchen of the homestead cabin, a doorway led to a small cozy living room that also served as a bedroom for Uncle Louie. In the left corner was Uncle Louie's polished brass bed with its high bedstead at the east wall. Its posts were topped by large brass spherical knobs finished off with fancy finial shapes. The foot of the bed had a horizontal rail high enough for my brother Ross when a young child to perform some little acrobatic stunts. The bed was always neatly made up with a Hudson Bay wool blanket that had broad colorful stripes, a favorite style used by frontiersmen who traded with the Indians. The bed was used for extra seating since there was no sofa or davenport in the room. In the right hand corner behind the door was Uncle Louie's space for hanging his good wool shirts on a tightly stretched rope fastened from the door at an angle across the corner.

Next to Uncle Louie's bed was an east window partially covered with ivy vines, giving a view of the farmyard with the well pump, milk house, big red barn, and corrals. Between 1946 and 1947, the big red barn with hay loft and cupola on the gambrel roof had been purchased by Uncles Emanuel and Louie, hauled in, and set up on the east side of the farm yard above the Buffalo Paunch Creek. When the barn was freshly set up before filling the hay mow with hay, someone suggested that the Washburn community be invited to a barn dance which I recall attending when I was about 13. The summer I worked for Grandma, and on other occasions, I remember how wonderful it was to enter the shadowy coolness of the big barn and walk down the wide center aisle inhaling the sweet fragrance of clover hay, the smell of the horses, and even their manure, which I didn't find offensive. Uncle Emanuel's huge team of draft horses would be in their stalls munching hay. Uncle Louie often had a spirited stallion in a box stall, stomping about and giving a shrill whinny. A stairs led up to the hay loft, where piles of loose meadow hay were stored and forked down through special holes in the floor next to the walls above the mangers below.

My brother Ross recalls memories of that day in October 1964 when the old homestead cabin burned. An old horseman, who was partially blind from his earlier career as a lightweight boxer, had come by to visit Uncle Louie. He was provided lodging and food. The old fellow, wanting to be helpful, had helped with dishes and cleaning up before Uncle Louie took him up to Underwood to catch a bus. When Uncle Louie returned an hour or more later, he found the cabin in smoldering ruin. It was surmised that the visitor, in cleaning up, perhaps had laid a dish towel on a lit burner on a small electric stove that had been installed in the kitchen. As Uncle Louie stared in a daze at the smoldering embers, he remarked to friends and family, "Well, I just as well could have worn those good wool shirts I was saving." This sentiment could be felt about many things we are saving for the future and not enjoying them in the present.

Following our return from Ecuador in the summer of 1972, Byron, the children and I visited my family in North Dakota. After our years of absence, the children had grown and we were reacquainting them with their grandparents,

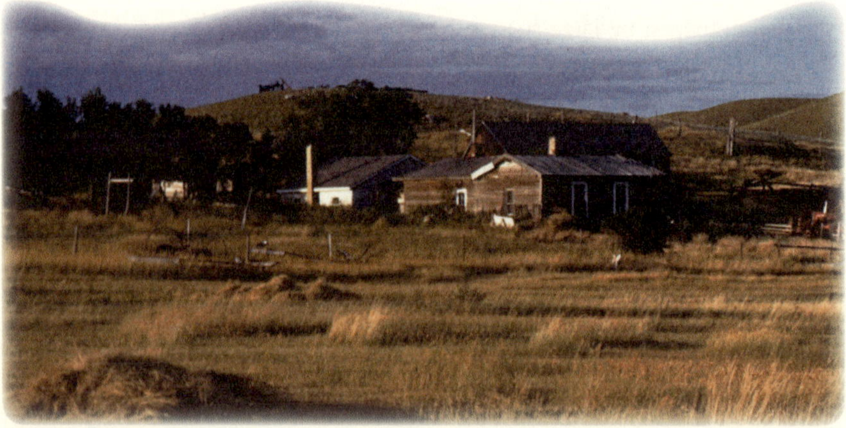

uncles, aunts and cousins. The old homestead was no longer the same; Grandma Martha and Uncle Emmanuel were no longer living. Uncle Louie now lived in a small one-room house he had hauled into the farm yard, after the homestead cabin burned. He still raised his greyhounds and had a young black male puppy that was a few months old. The children fell in love with the pup. Just as Uncle Louie treated my siblings and me with attention and gifts, he extended his generosity to his great-nieces and great-nephews. So, Uncle Louie gave the puppy to them. The children were thrilled with the gift and named him "Zorro."

Zorro adjusted well to his 1200 mile trip by car to his new home back in Indiana and became a great companion of the children. The following April, wild mushroom season was at its height in the woods on our farm in Indiana. Morels, an edible wild mushroom, grow in the woods – seemingly springing up overnight from nowhere. They are well disguised -- their coloring blended with last year's dry brown leaves covering the forest floor.

Morels are a very much sought after delicacy. When soaked in salt water, rolled in flour and fried, they are most delicious. It is, therefore, a spring ritual for locals to go "mushroom hunting". People who take their mushroom hunting seriously keep their prized "mushroom" locations a well-guarded secret. Byron would take the children mushroom hunting on a favorite wooded hillside on Harmony Hill. He taught them the technique for best locating mushrooms by standing perfectly still, staring at the surrounding ground covering of leaves and twigs until suddenly, as if by magic, the shape of a mushroom seemed to spring into view.

One day in April, we suddenly noticed that our daughter, Maria, (about 7 years old) was gone and no one knew where she was. We became alarmed,

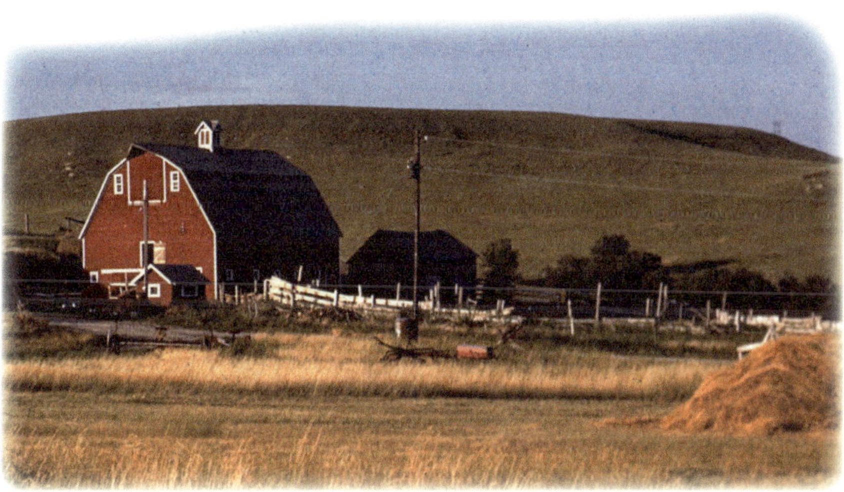

after searching and calling for her with no success. We notified nearby neighbors and relatives that Maria was missing. We were concerned, because our property adjoined thousands of acres of the Clark State Forestry, and Maria, having not lived there long, was not familiar with the layout of the property. Just as we were about to send out a search party, Maria appeared carrying a little basket filled with mushrooms with Zorro trotting at her side. Maria was so proud of all the mushrooms she found. She said that Zorro sniffed the mushrooms out from among the leaves and debris, helping her locate them. To this day, mushroom hunting has held a fascination for Maria, and she is proud of her big 'finds'.

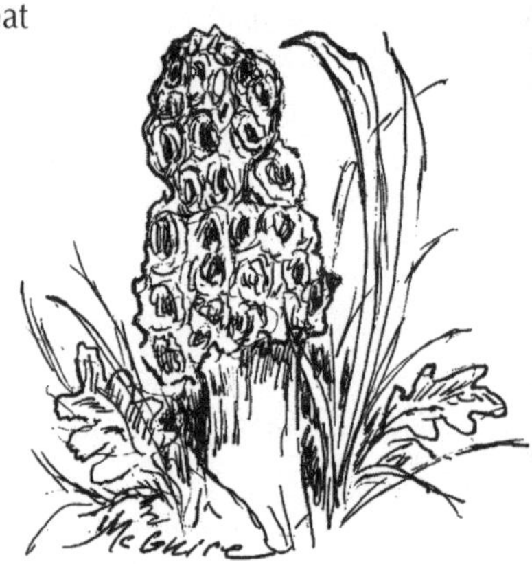

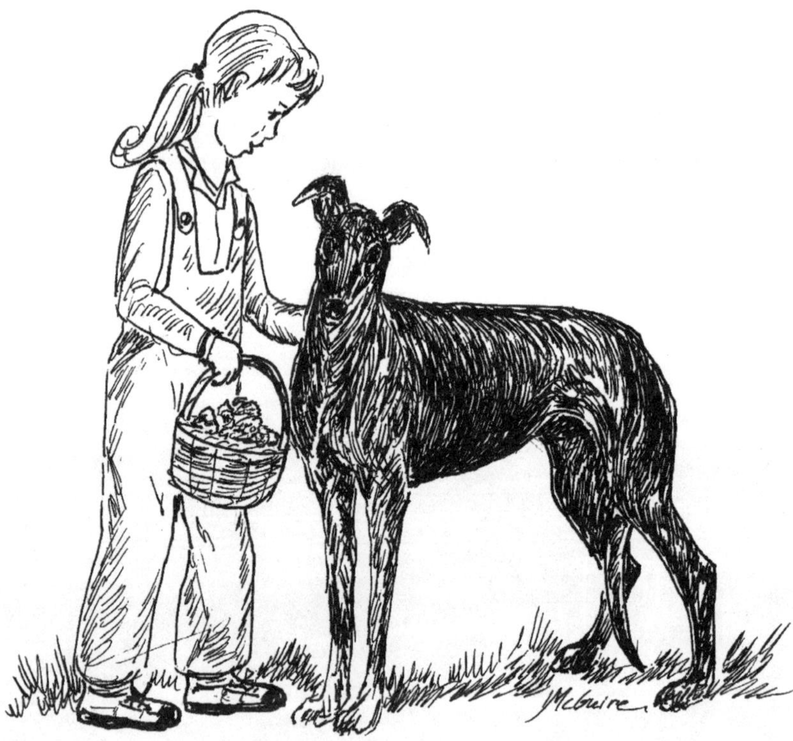

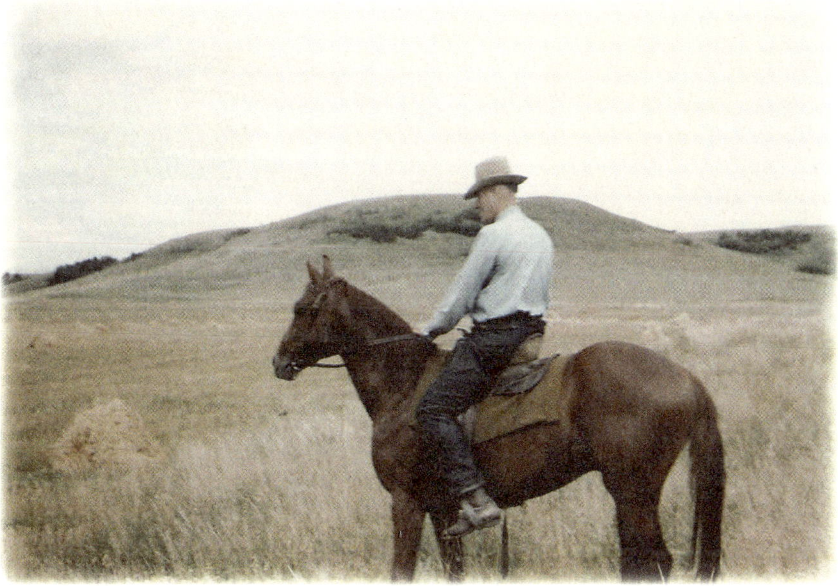

LOUIE LORENTZEN

That summer when Uncle Louie gave us Zorro I believe was the last time we saw him alive. He passed away in August 1973 at the age of 76. In my father's notes I found these simple words he wrote about his brother Louie: "Loved children, horseman-cowboy."

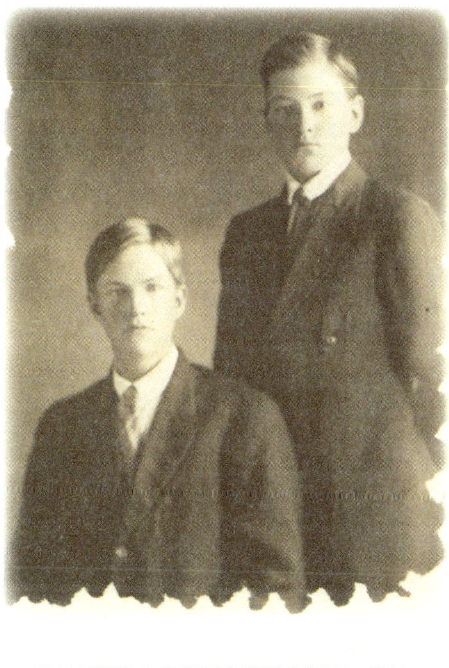

EMANUEL & LOUIE LORENTZEN - 1914

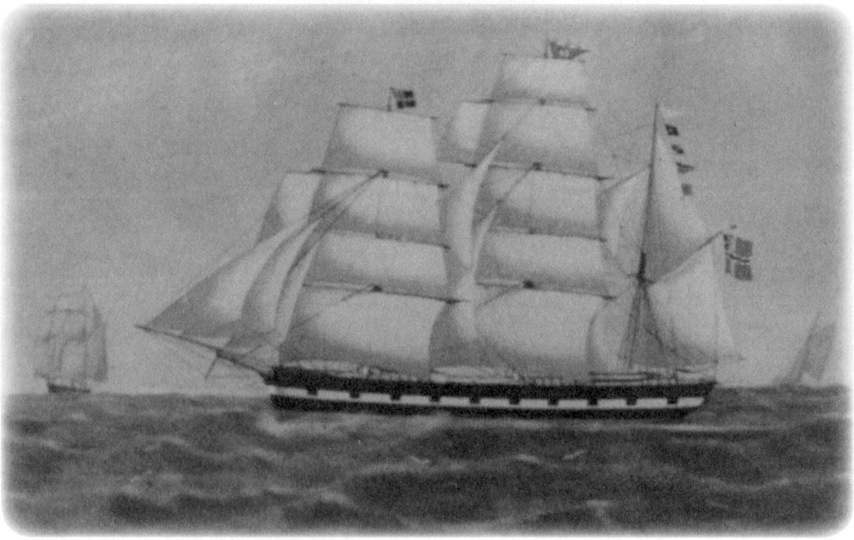

"THE NOAH OF CHRISTIANSANDE"
(PHOTO OF ORIGINAL WATER COLOR PAINTING)
CAPTAIN EMANUEL LORENTZEN

CHAPTER 7

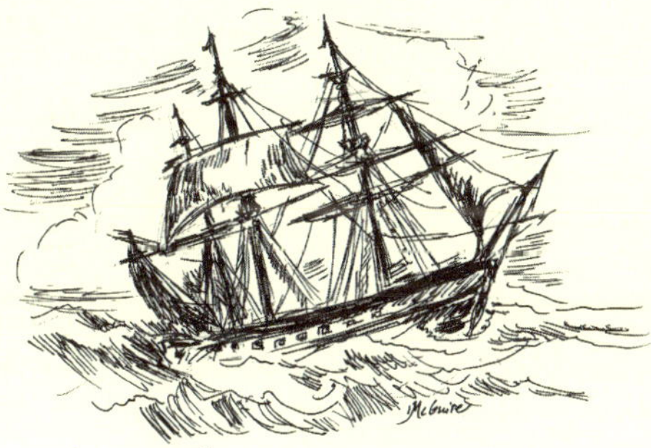

The Noah

In the living room of the homestead cabin, next to the east window overlooking the barnyard was a round oak pedestal table with a kerosene lamp in the middle, surrounded by several issues of **The Bismarck Tribune** and **LIFE** magazine, which Uncle Emanuel subscribed to and read in the evenings when his work was finished. I also enjoyed reading these since I didn't have them in my home. Around the table was another chair or two and a rocking chair. Reading at the table after dark, a golden circle of lamplight shone upon the table, casting flickering shadows in the corners of the room. In the middle of the right west wall was a large coal-burning heating stove with a coal bucket next to it. The soft lignite coal was hauled by pickup truck from a coal mine a few miles away and stored in a sloped roofed shed attached to the north end of the cabin.

Across the room a south window let in sunshine, a view of the grassy yard, and a lilac bush. Beyond the wooded bottom land a glimpse of the distant Missouri River could be seen shining like a narrow ribbon through the cottonwood trees. A bench beneath the window held a few potted red geraniums and pink begonias adding color and cheer to the room. Cared for year-round, they revealed my grandma's love for plants and beauty, and must have been especially appreciated when the snow piled high around the cabin and the storm-driven winds whistled and howled around the windows.

The focal point in the living room was on the southeast wall, where I would stand in awe before the large original watercolor painting of a big sailing ship, its white sails billowing in the wind, and colorful flags flying. Choppy blue ocean waves smoothed out in the distance to meet the White Cliffs of Dover. Beneath the painting was the inscription, ***Noah of Christiansande, Captain Emanuel Lorentzen.*** The painting was done in 1868 by Andre Lind, a Swedish wharf artist in London, while great-grandfather's ship was in the British Channel during one of his frequent trips across the Atlantic from Norway to the British Isles transporting various cargo. From my father's notes he wrote that 18 voyages from Norway to the United States, and Quebec, Canada had been made. Voyages had also taken them into the Mediterranean Sea.

In his handwritten notes made in 1958, my father Henry said that **The Noah of Christiansand** was a freighter with three masts, built in Holland in the 1800's, the exact year is uncertain. **The Noah's** captain, Emanuel Lorentzen, had a home in the small coastal village of Lillesand, Norway, where he and his family maintained a white-framed warehouse and small store in their home port. At the time of my father's writing, he thought these buildings near the wharf were possibly still standing. Dealing mainly in staple foods, **The Noah** sailed to different ports in Europe including voyages to Odessa Russia on the Black Sea, bringing cargoes of rye. Emanuel's son, Lorentz, served as the Captain's mate, although he too had a captain's credentials.

I find it fascinating to try tracing the travel routes my grandfather Lorentz and great-grandfather Emanuel sailed on **The Noah**. In my mind's eye I picture

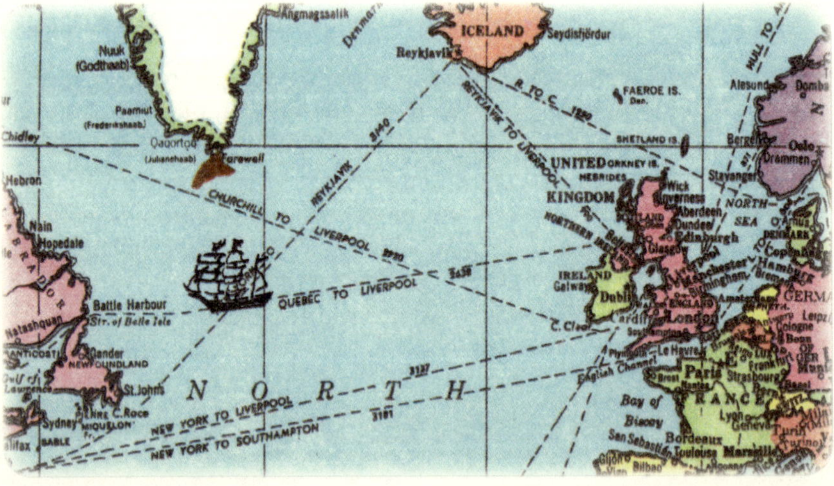

the busy seaports, foreign people and strange lands they encountered. Using a magnifying glass and a world atlas, I study maps imagining them setting sail from the wharf in Lillesand Norway, sailing south across the North Sea to pass through the Strait of Dover, the English Channel, across the Bay of Biscay in the Atlantic Ocean, sailing past Spain and Portugal to enter the Strait of Gibraltar and on into the Mediterranean Sea. Navigating past the shores of North Africa, through the Sea of Crete and on into the Aegean Sea to enter the Dardanelles, and the Sea of Marmara, they at last sailed through the narrow neck guarded by the ancient city of Istanbul into the Black Sea to finally reach the port of Odessa to take on cargo of rye.

Surrounding the ship picture was a tragic story and unsolved mystery that haunts me to this day. Great-Grandfather Captain Emanuel Lorentzen and his son Lorentz had crossed the Atlantic to America with cargo and were preparing to return with the ship reloaded with cargo to Norway. Lorentz decided to stay in America and make his way down the St. Lawrence River and through the Great Lakes to find work as a shipbuilder and not return this trip to Norway. Another version of the story was that he was sick and stayed in Montreal. For whatever reason, he stayed, and his father, Captain Emanuel, and his crew started their homeward journey back to Norway in November 1882.

I try to picture that last farewell: a father and son who had shared so many voyages together, telling each other goodbye with a manly embrace and parting words about when they may expect to meet again. I can see Lorentz standing on the shore, watching ***The Noah*** slowly sail out of the harbor. Captain Emanuel, having trained his son from a young cabin boy on up, may have had visions of stepping aside to have his son Lorentz one day stand at the helm. They may have, however, considered the possibility that Lorentz's stay in America could be permanent. During that time, many Norwegians were immigrating to the United States looking for free homestead land in the West and hopefully a better more prosperous life.

My father Henry said there were two versions of the last sighting of ***The Noah***. One was that the ship and crew were last seen off the coast of Newfoundland and were shipwrecked in a terrible storm never to be seen again. The other story was that the ship was found empty of cargo and crew so that pirates on the high seas were suspected. I can visualize the storm-tossed sea, the creaking ship, the roar of the icy wind and the driving rain and sleet in their faces as they struggled to secure the ship.

To clarify the disappearance of ***The Noah***, my father wrote the following letter addressed to his cousin Kjell Rosenberg in Lillesand, Norway:

Washburn, N.D.
April 15, 1988

Dear Kjell:

I failed to mention an important fact in regard to the final voyage of the "Noah of Christiansand", Grandfather Emanuel Lorentzen's ship. Before returning, Grandfather Emanuel decided to make one more long voyage so he sailed to Quebec, Canada. His son Lorentz went along as mate, but he too had a captain's credentials. This was in the early eighties and the first part of November. Lorentz stayed in Quebec for the time being and his father left port with the Noah bound for Liverpool and home.

Now this is the true story that was handed down by my father Lorentz. About two weeks after the Noah had left port, a very severe storm swept the North Atlantic, and it was assumed that the Noah was so battered and wrecked it sank with its crew. Also for the record the Noah was loaded mainly with sugar and other goods for the forthcoming Christmas season. As father and son parted there at Quebec, it was understood that Lorentz was to establish a home in America, and even Grandfather considered doing the same, but Grandmother Ragnhild didn't favor the idea. A son-in-law (Jerry Vonderheide) who travels to Norway and other countries visited a Museum of Maritime History on the island near Oslo and there he was given a copy of the Noah's inspection record.

The Andersons, Knudtsons and my folks all agree that it was as I have written and not a scrap or bit of the Noah and crew were ever found. Please pardon this hasty letter, perhaps you could type it over.

With love to all,
Cousin Henry
Lorentzen

Post Script (over)

Just another interesting bit... In his bunk aboard ship, Grandfather slept upon a reindeer skin among other covers, and am sure he had a good sized feather bed. The folks called a feer duena, which is as best I can spell it.

As a further tribute to the man, I will mention the many stories that the relationships would tell about this most generous and kind man.

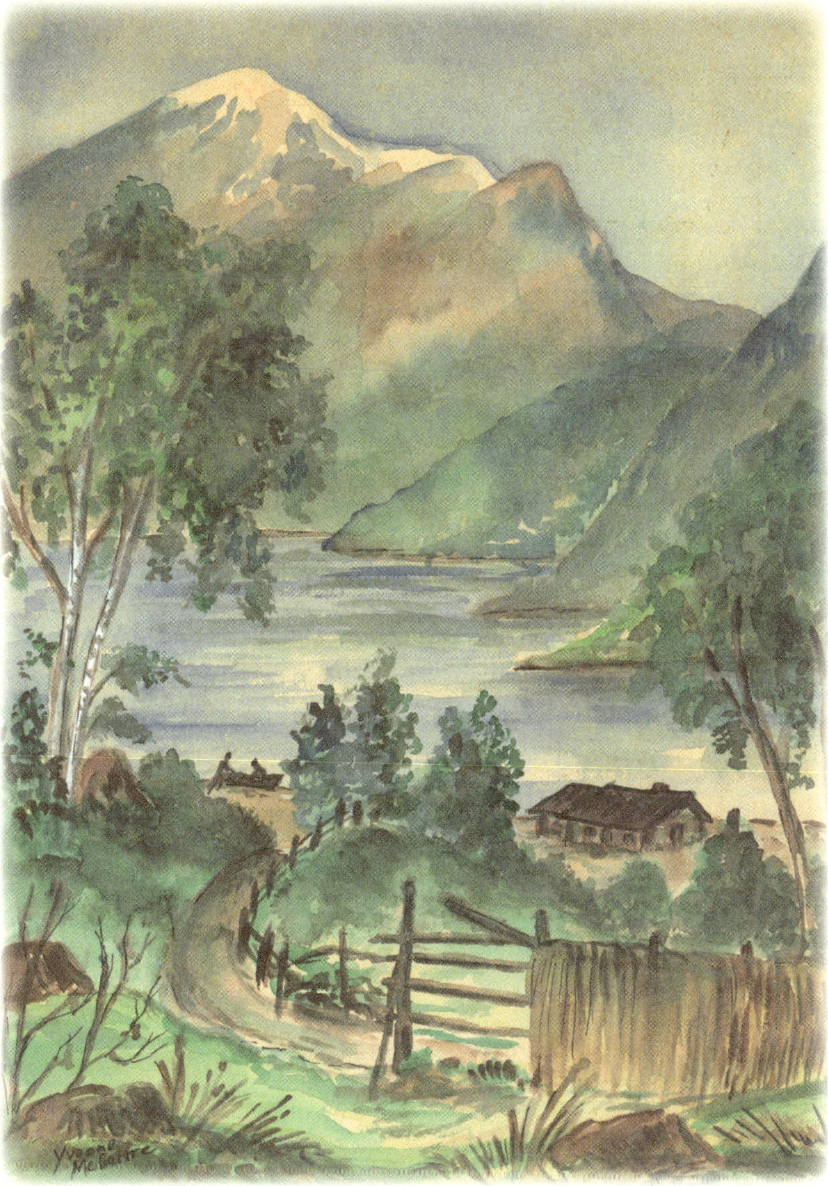

"FJORD OF NORWAY"
WATERCOLOR BY YVONNE LORENTZEN MCGUIRE

What a vigil it must have been for the women and children to watch and wait for the safe return of their men from each long voyage. And then, what a time of rejoicing it would be to see the long-awaited ship sail into the harbor. Grandmother Martha told me how Captain Emanuel's wife, Ragnhild, and their daughters use to cut some of their long hair to weave with yarn into mittens to give them extra warmth for the men's hands, when they would be out on the cold wet sea. The human hair woven with the wool also helped prevent shrinkage of the wet mittens. Grandma said that one of Captain Emanuel's daughters who had especially beautiful long hair was reluctant to have her hair cut off, but when she was reminded of how it would help her father keep warm out on the cold sea, she willingly agreed to cut her hair.

Word had been received from America that ***The Noah*** would be returning to its native land of Norway, laden with cargo and special gifts for the women and children. With no modern means of communication, it must have been nearly unbearable as weeks, perhaps months, slipped by, waiting for the return of the ship. I can only imagine the long weeks of anxiety and worry the womenfolk endured as they awaited the safe return of a husband, son, brother, or lover. Did their mountainside home overlook the sea? Were their eyes continually searching for the distant approach on the horizon of a ship? As it drew nearer, could they identify the ship with its flags unfurled, sailing safely into the harbor? What indescribable grief and sorrow gripped their hearts when they finally realized there was no hope of seeing their loved ones again – no joyous homecoming.

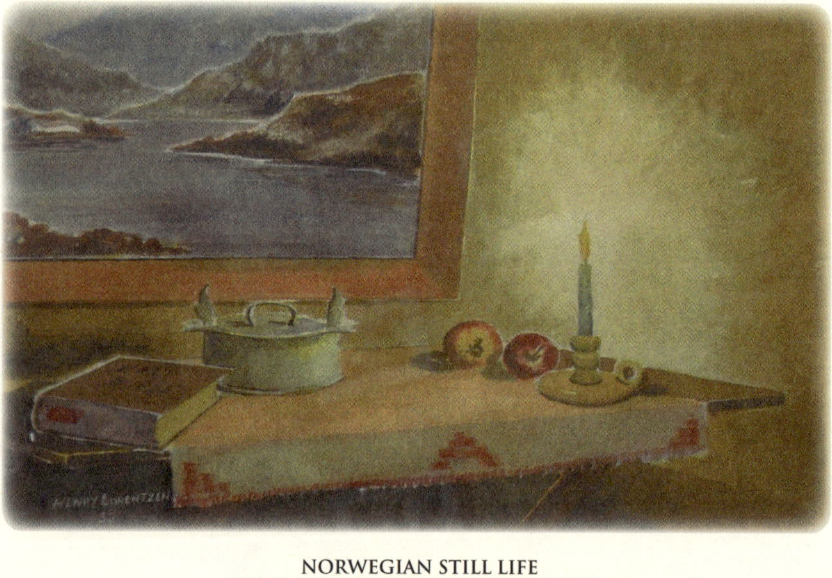

NORWEGIAN STILL LIFE
WATERCOLOR BY HENRY LORENTZEN

Cousin Kjell Rosenberg in his book, "The Loentzen Saga" said: "As the years passed, Captain Lorentzen wanted to settle on shore and had bought a farm on the mainland in 1871. To raise more money for purchase of the farm – Fleseid – he wanted to make another trip with ***The Noah*** that sailed for Canada. This became his last voyage."

Captain Emanuel's widow, my great-grandmother Ragnhild, who I was never to know, had not only lost her husband but also her brother, Knud Gundersen on ***The Noah***. She took care of the family farm with the help of her daughters. In Rosenberg's writing he says, "She had some cattle and sheep and made a living out of the farm being self-supporting as possible. Probably Lorentz sent her some money from the states. Her daughters went to school on Äkerøya." Ragnhild lived on the farm Fleseid nearly up to her death in 1903. In her old age she sold the farm and lived her last years in Gamle Hellesund with her daughter Elizabeth Knudsen (Knutson). Ragnhild's only living son, Lorentz Lorentzen, had stayed in America, married and settled with his wife Martha on their North Dakota homestead. After Ragnhild's passing in Norway, Lorentz managed to save enough money to send to his widowed sister, Elizabeth Knutson, so she and her six children could come to America to settle on a nearby homestead in 1903. Her husband had also been lost at sea.

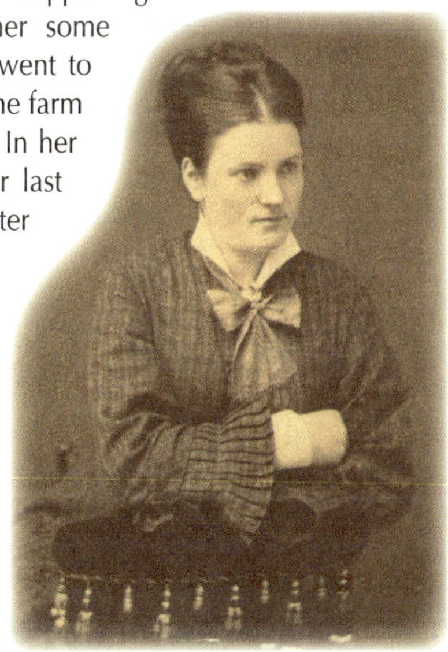

ELISABETH (AUNTIE LISA) KNUDTSON

In Norway the painting of ***The Noah*** no doubt had hung in a prominent place on the wall of the Lorentzen farm home. The painting was taken down from its honored place in the old family home in Norway, and was carefully wrapped and placed at the bottom of a sea chest going to America with the Knutsons. The family probably reasoned that the rightful one to inherit the painting should be Lorentz, the only living son of the Captain, who had made so many voyages with his father on ***The Noah***. After traveling thousands of miles over the storm-tossed ocean, perhaps going by railroad for hundreds of miles, and then bouncing over many bumpy, rough roads in a horse-drawn wagon, the family's prized possession finally came to the end of its journey to be hung upon the wall of the humble homestead cabin on the lonely windswept prairie of North Dakota.

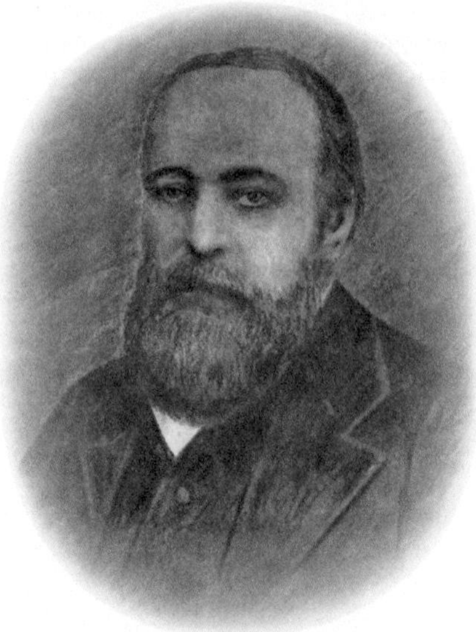

CAPTAIN EMANUEL LORENTZEN
1819-1882

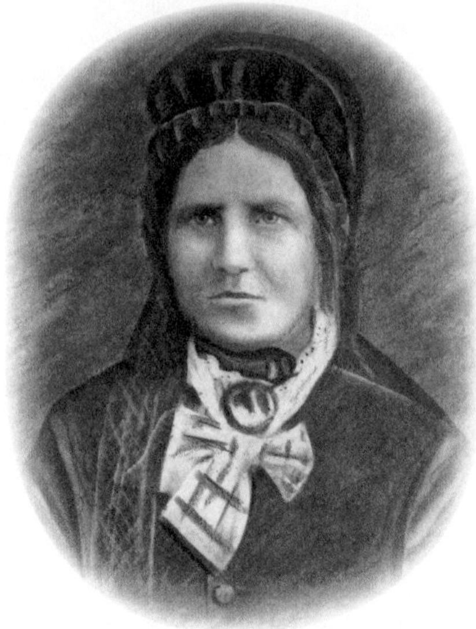

RAGNHILD LORENTZEN
1822-1903

To stand before the framed ship painting hanging on the wall in my grandma's log home gave me a sense of pride. Though we were poor by worldly standards, we possessed a family treasure that no one else around, even in the finest homes, could claim. So I grew up proud to be an American, but proud of my Norwegian heritage. I always felt a thrill of pride to know I descended from such courageous, adventuresome men, my grandfather Lorentz Lorentzen born in 1850 in Norway, son of my great-grandfather Captain Emanuel Lorentzen, son of my great-great grandfather Captain Lorentz Ellefsen, from the beautiful port city of Lillisand, Norway, all whom had piloted various ships plying the high seas. Standing before the painting, I could feel the call of the sea racing in my own blood. Could there be something inherited from generations of seamen dating back to the Vikings? It was told that when Uncle Emanuel crossed the ocean to France in World War I, he was the only one aboard the ship who didn't get seasick. Is it possible that such an adaptation to a rolling ship could be inherited from generations of seafaring ancestors? One could understand the magnetic pull to sail the high seas and hoist the billowing sails in the wind. It must be something akin to the pulling force which whispers to the wild geese, "Spring is in the air; it's time to fly North."

Pride in ***The Noah*** and our rich heritage was shared by most of the members of my family, including, of course, my father Henry. My father had become a well-recognized artist having been named North Dakota's "Artist of the Year" in 1957. Thankfully, he replicated the painting of ***The Noah*** before the old cabin burned in 1964, destroying its wealth of family treasures and the precious original. My father's 24″ X 36″ oil painting of ***The Noah*** became one of his most prized works of art. My brother, Norman Emanuel, inherited the painting after our father passed away in 1997. He in turn gave the painting to his daughter, Holly Reid.

Beneath the ship picture within the homestead cabin, sat a large wooden sideboard or buffet with drawers and bottom doors for storage. That summer, while helping Grandma Martha, I had time to browse through some of the old papers stored there. I discovered Grandmother Martha saved newspaper clippings about various things that interested her, such as articles and pictures about the Queen of England and world events. Though she was isolated on a prairie homestead, she took a keen interest in the outside world. I also came across papers with long, hand-written mathematical calculations so complicated and far beyond my high school math and algebra. Grandma told me these were made by Grandpa Lorentz using the compass and position of stars in the navigation of the ship. From this, I knew my grandfather must have been a very intelligent and skilled man, beyond what I could comprehend.

My cousin Lorentz Lorentzen, son of Uncle Osborne and Aunt Blanche, recalled as a boy visiting Grandma Martha and Uncle Louie and Uncle Emanuel in their old log home. He too browsed through the old cupboard beneath the ship painting and suddenly was surprised to hold a document with his own name, Lorentz Lorentzen, inscribed on it, certifying that the bearer of that name was a licensed captain of any ship in the United States Navy. It was then he realized what an honor it was to be the namesake and grandson of such a distinguished man.

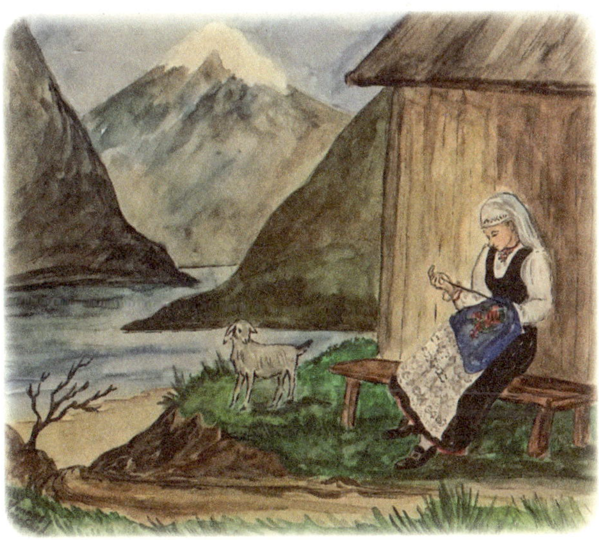

"NORWEGIAN GIRL SEWING NEEDLE POINT"
WATERCOLOR PAINTING BY YVONNE MCGUIRE

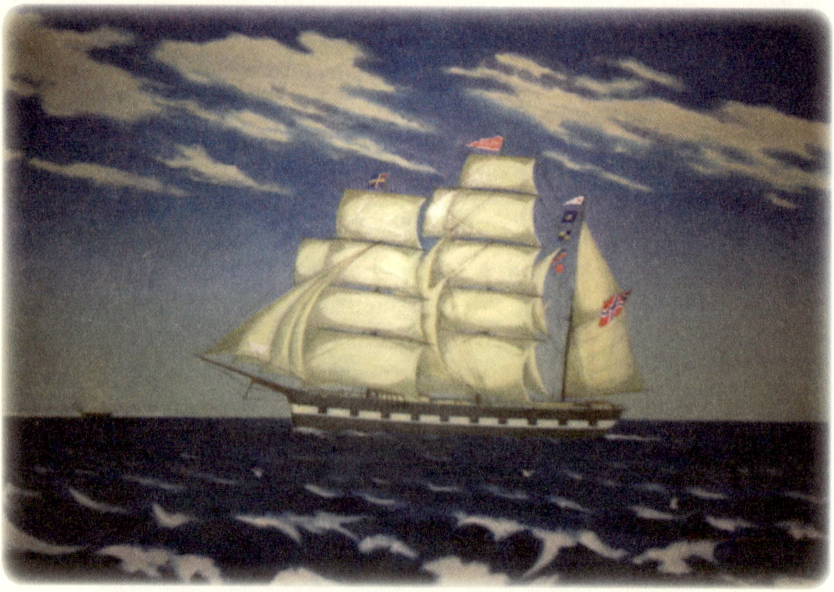

"THE NOAH"
OIL PAINTING BY HENRY LORENTZEN

Kjell Rosenberg in his writing ***The Lorentzen Saga***, uses the expression, "sailed down" to indicate those who drowned in shipwrecks or sailing disasters. Somehow the term seems to soften the tragedy of their death. My niece, Vanessa Lorentzen, gave the following reading at the funeral of my father, Henry Lorentzen, in January 1997. Though he passed away on the frozen prairie of North Dakota, far from the home of his Norwegian seafaring ancestors, it seemed so appropriate.

A Parable of Immortality

I am standing upon the seashore. A ship at my side spreads her white sails to the morning breeze and starts for the blue ocean. She is an object of beauty and strength.

I stand and watch her, until at length; she hangs like a speck, a white cloud, just where the sea and sky come to mingle with each other.

Then someone at my side says: "There, she is gone!"
"Gone where?"
Gone from my sight. That is all.

She is just as large in mast and hull and spar, as she was when she left my side, and she is just as able to bear her load of living freight to her destined port.

Her diminished size is in me, not in her. And just at the moment when someone at my side says: "There, she is gone!" There are other eyes watching her coming, and other voices ready to take up the glad shout: "Here she comes!"

And that is dying.

~Henry Van Dyke

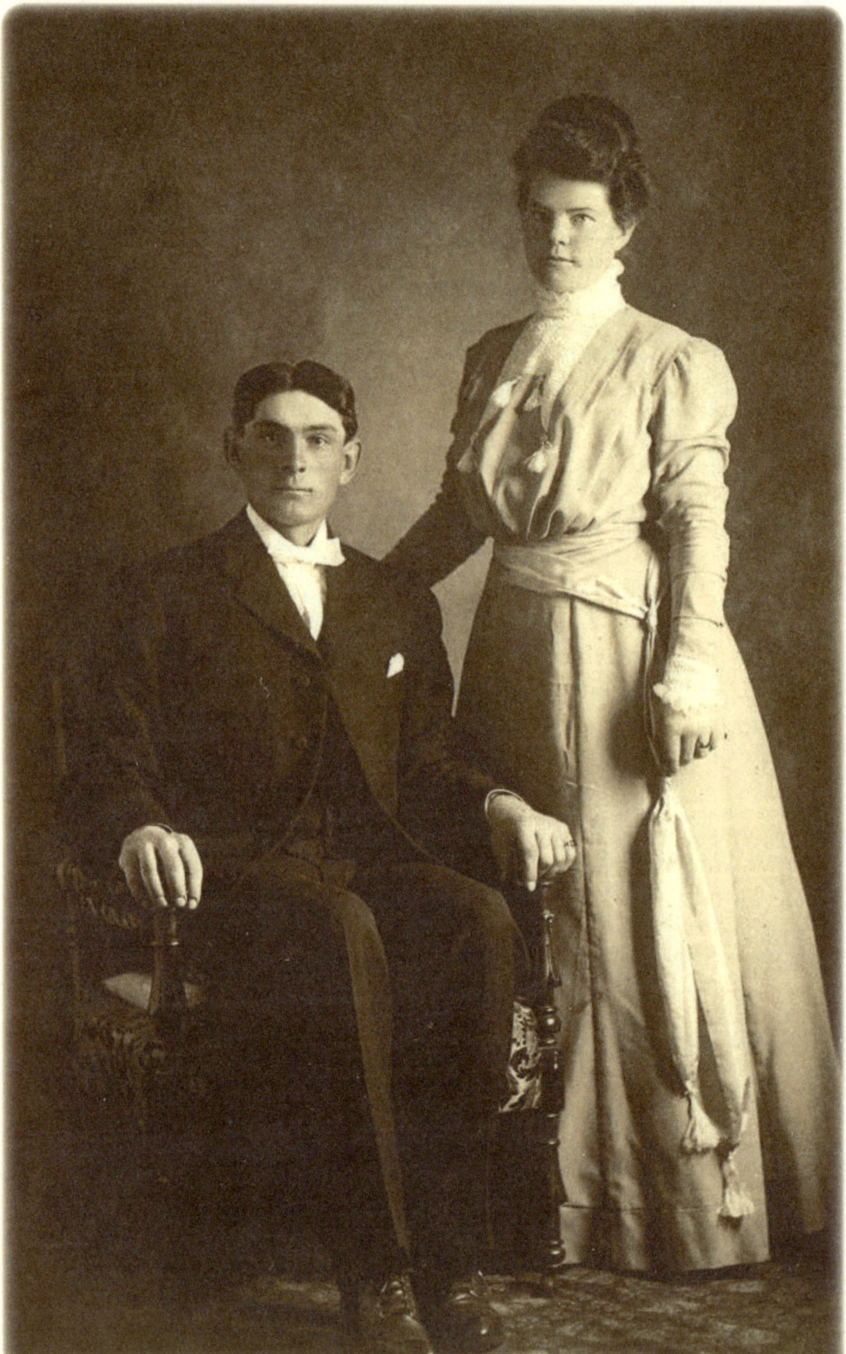

WEDDING OF JOHN BUKACEK & EDNA LORENTZEN IN 1909

CHAPTER 8

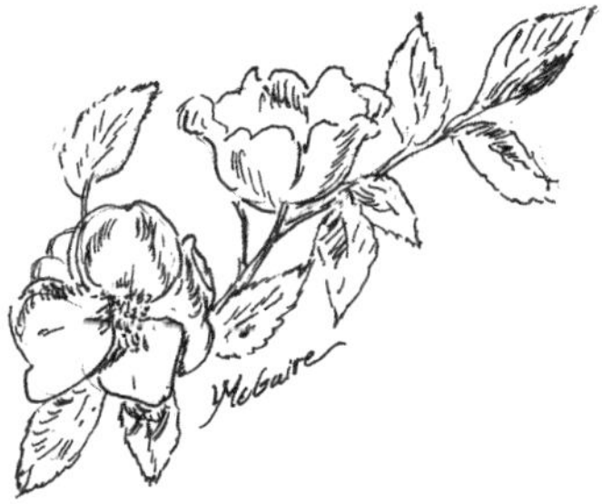

Sister Edna

To the right of the sunny south living room window was a tall antique combination desk and bookcase, with a curved glass door on the left, revealing shelves of well-used books. On the right side was a hinged wood door that dropped down to serve as a writing desk, with compartments or pigeon holes above for writing materials and correspondence. There were a few things displayed on the top, which I can't exactly remember, but I recall a vase of three or four deep red poinsettia flowers made of felt or velvet. Also, there was a seashell that Grandma had us children hold to our ears so we could listen to the distant sound of the ocean within it. Perhaps Grandpa Lorentz had picked it up on a faraway foreign seashore on one of his voyages.

On the wall near the desk was a gold oval-framed portrait of a beautiful young woman with an abundance of rich brown hair swept high on her head in the fashionable Gibson Girl style of the times. Her innocent clear luminous eyes seemed to hold your gaze. She wore a high-necked blouse with a bit of lace clasped at the throat with a brooch and a deep burgundy jumper. She was my father's beloved oldest sister, Edna, who was like a second mother to him, when he was a young child. My father Henry said, "Sister Edna was the one person who really understood me." She possessed such inner beauty of spirit, as well as outward beauty in her loving helpful ways. She was adored by all. Grandma told me how beautiful Edna was and what a willing, quick worker she was. She carefully cared for her clothing and was fussy about washing her long hair ribbons, which she stylishly wore in big bows in her upswept hair. Grandma said that one day Edna had washed her hair ribbons and hung them out on the clothesline to dry in the sun. She happened to look out the window in time to see the old milk cow swallowing one of the ribbons off the clothesline. Quick as a wink, Edna ran out, thrust her hand down the cow's throat, and pulled out the ribbon, finding it not much the worse for wear.

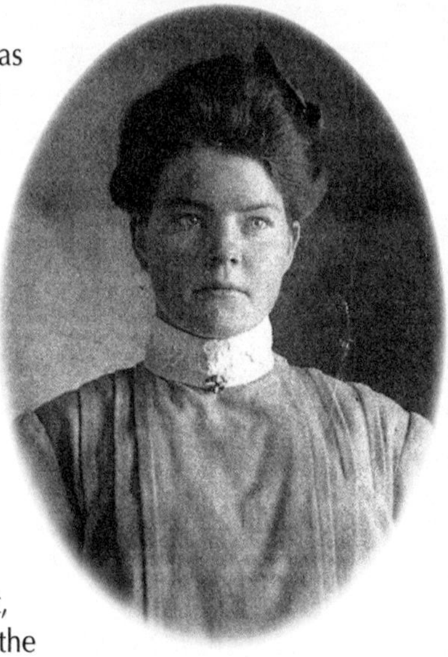

EDNA ROSANNA LORENTZEN

As a young girl, my eyes were always drawn to this lovely portrait. I wished that I somehow could be as beautiful. Sometimes I stood before a mirror, holding my hair on top of my head, looking for some resemblance to Edna. Tragedy and mystery seemed to surround her.

Edna Rosanna Lorentzen was born on September 14, 1886 and in her early twenties married John Bukacek. My father said that John and his parents had immigrated to Nebraska from Bohemia, later known as Czechoslovakia. Among my father's treasured keepsakes was Edna and John's wedding photo taken by Degraff at Washburn, ND in the early part of 1909. On the back of the photo, he wrote that Edna had sewed her wedding dress of a gray-tan material and that she also sewed a matching dress for her china doll. She made a pretty little wig for the doll from her own brown hair, fashioned in a style similar to her own. My sister Estell, when she was about twelve or thirteen years old, was given this precious doll by Grandma Martha. Estell said that Grandma had tears in her eyes as she presented the doll. The doll, made in Germany, was beautiful with a delicate porcelain face and hands and blue glass eyes. The doll's carefully tailored suit of soft dove gray had a silk bodice with a tiny agate pin clasped at its lacy neck.

I don't remember hearing the story of how Edna and John met, but my father told me of an incident of when his sisters Edna and Estella were bringing up the milk cows from the Buffalo Paunch Creek, a young stranger came riding by, and stopped to sing to them, "Two Little Girls in Blue Land", and "Sweet Bunch of Daisies Brought From the Dell." These must have been popular songs from the late 1800's. I don't know if he could possibly have been John. My cousin Karen Lorentzen, daughter of Uncle Haldor, said that Grandma Martha rented a room above Holtan's Mercantile so Estella and Edna could stay there to attend school in Washburn. Boarding there made it possible for them to continue their education when bad weather and impassable roads would have prevented their traveling by horse and buggy from their homestead home. Estella worked at the Leader office with Editor Joseph Henry Taylor to help pay for their room and board. Cousin Karen said there were dances held in the old hotel where the girls may have enjoyed some social life. Maybe John met Edna there.

Edna and John farmed a small homestead about seven miles east of Turtle Lake, North Dakota. At that time my father was almost nine years old and had spent some time with Edna and John in their homestead house. He slept in a small wooden bed built in the corner of the house. Edna and John were expecting their first child. When Edna went into premature labor, she experienced difficulties. The doctor was late in arriving, presumably celebrating Independence Day. When he eventually came, he was under the influence of alcohol. After a difficult birthing, she and her newborn infant tragically died on July 4, 1909.

While the Lorentzen family felt the deep loss of Edna, there is the untold story of her young husband John, who must have suffered great grief and pain to lose his beautiful wife and their baby. I wondered what became of him. Did he stay in North Dakota to labor alone on his prairie homestead to "prove up" or complete the requirements for claiming ownership so his and Edna's labors would not be in vain? But without Edna at his side, could he endure the lonely, dark nights when stormy winds howled around their humble shanty?

On the day of Edna's funeral, my father said he, as a nine-year-old boy, rode with John on the seat of the wagon that carried Edna's casket to the Riverview cemetery in Washburn. Edna's favorite little horse helped pull the wagon. My father said that after the funeral, John got on a train to return to his original home in Nebraska. I always wondered if John was able to rebuild his life there and eventually find love and happiness again. My cousin Karen recalls hearing from Uncle Louie that John did return once a year in the fall for a while and would bring candy in the large pockets of his overcoat for his wife Edna's young brothers, but it always made their mother, Martha, cry to see him. So he eventually returned no more. I wish, that summer with my grandmother, I had asked her questions about this, but I avoided renewing old memories that would make her sad.

In looking through my father's keepsakes preserved in an old wooden box, I found a postcard of an old-world Santa Claus, dressed in a red suit covered with a cloth-like material that looks and feels like velvet to the touch. The Santa carries a small Christmas tree over his shoulder and on his back there is a bag filled with toys. Under one arm is a musical horn, a package, and a drum. The card is addressed in beautiful penmanship to "Henry Lorentzen, Washburn, North Dakota". The message reads, "Wish You a Merry Christmas and a Happy New Year From John E Bukacek".

The card, over one hundred years old, appears to be almost as new as the day received through the mail by my father. The postmark over the one-cent stamp clearly reads: "Clarkson, Nebr. Dec. 24 10 AM 1909." I think John had special feelings for his wife's nine-year-old brother who had spent time with them in their homestead home. No doubt he was missing Edna greatly as Christmas approached, and knew her little brother Henry was sadly missing her too.

My father felt the loss and grief of losing his sister Edna for the rest of his life. Many years later as a grown man, when he worked as a McLean County tax assessor, he was at the farm that had once been part of Edna and John's homestead and he located their old tumbled-down house and the little built-in bed was still there in the corner. At the age of 91, my father stood beside me in the little country New Chapel Church at Underwood, Indiana. As we sang "God Will Take Care of You", there was a catch in his voice and tears ran down his cheeks. Later, he told me that song was sung at his sister's funeral.

While writing this true story about my father's sister Edna and her husband John, I have found myself grieving over these dear people, who lived over a hundred years ago, as if I really knew them. In a sense, I felt I knew Edna from so often having studied her portrait hanging on the wall of the homestead cabin for so many years, and feeling the strong bond of love my father, his siblings, and their mother had for her.

My niece Vanessa Lorentzen shared my desire to know more about John and spent hours on the Internet researching his family history, his hometown in Nebraska, newspaper records, death and cemetery records. To our great disappointment, we found no happy ending. Following a nervous breakdown, he had been admitted to a mental institution, where he stayed until his death in 1942 at the age of 60. Our hopes were dashed to pieces at this finding, and it actually took time for me to regain enthusiasm to continue with my writing.

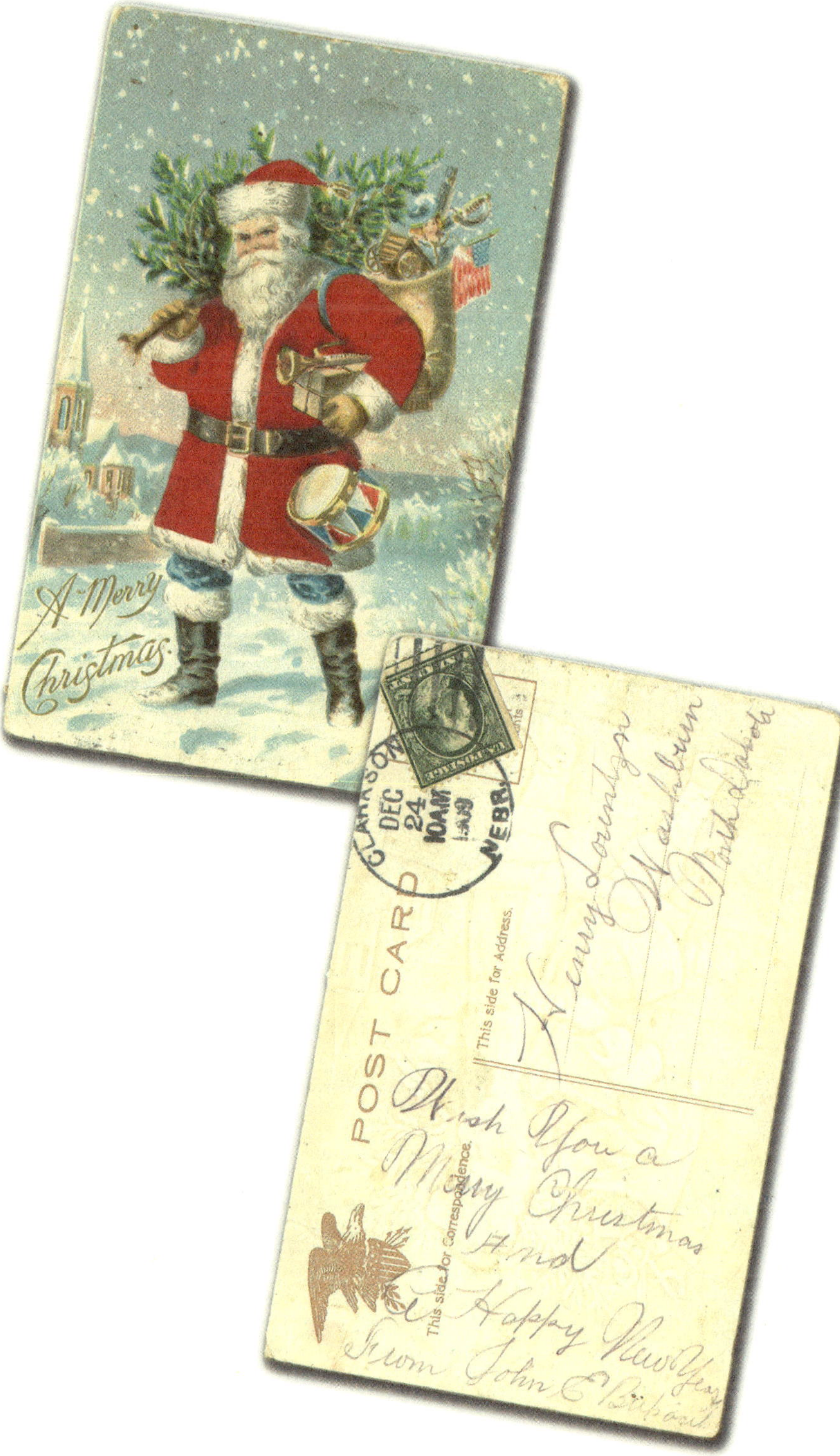
A Merry Christmas
POST CARD
This side for Address.
This side for Correspondence.
CLARKSON DEC 24 10AM NEBR.
Wish You a Merry Christmas And a Happy New Year From John E

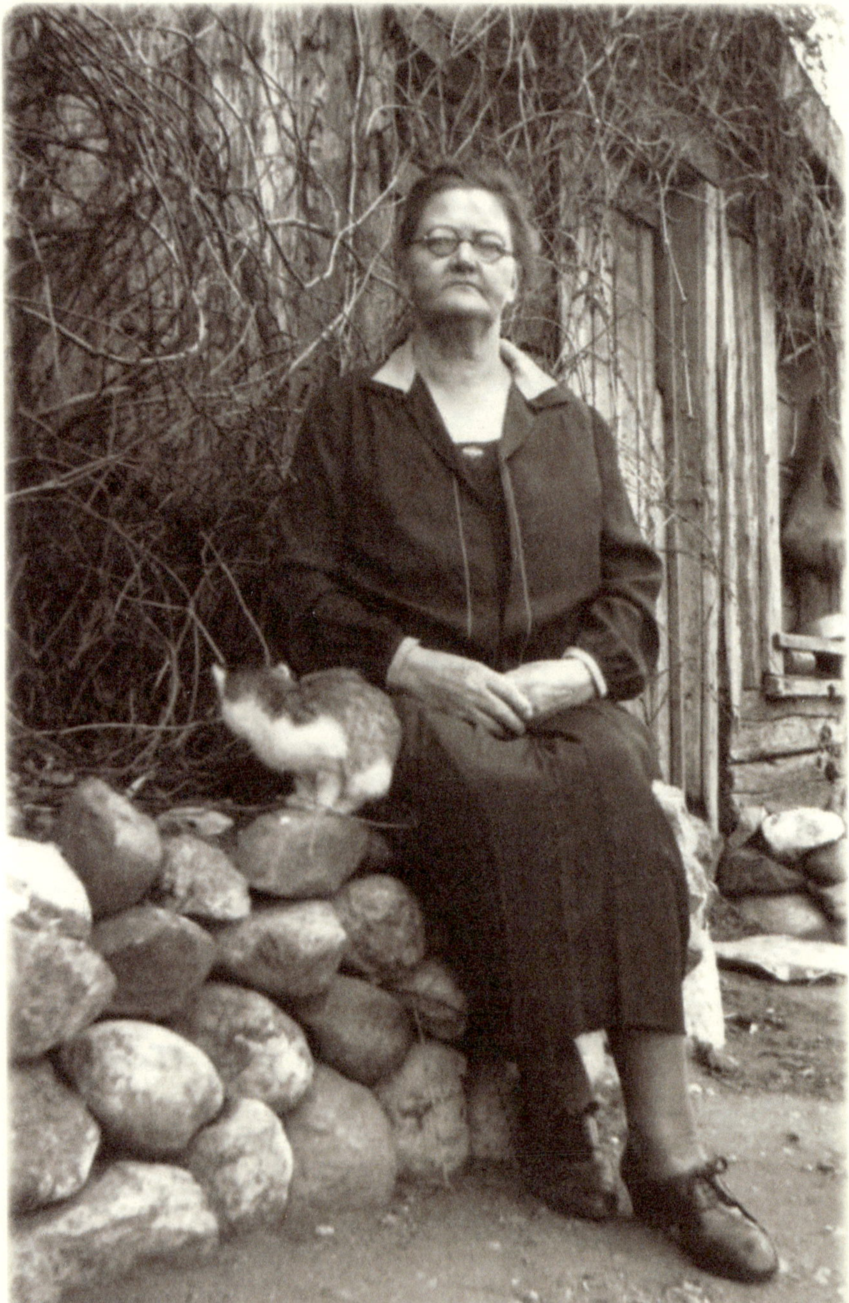

GRANDMA MARTHA LORENTZEN BY HOMESTEAD CABIN

CHAPTER 9

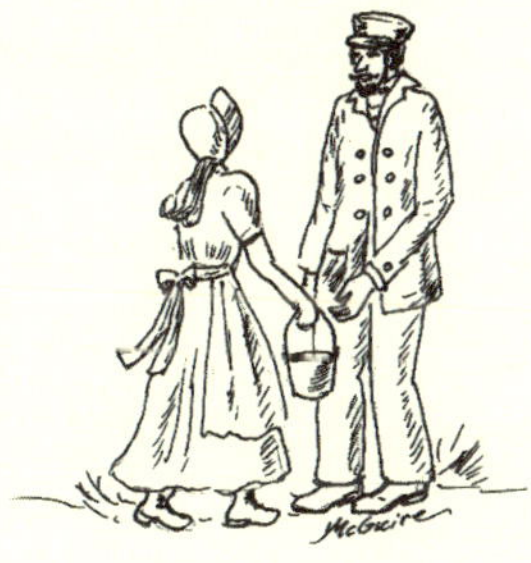

Grandma Martha & Family

On the west living room wall, next to the combination desk and bookcase, was the door to my Grandmother Martha's bedroom. In her room were two full-sized beds, a dresser and an old wooden Norwegian sea chest, with hand-painted lettering and a date that I cannot remember. The chest contained special linens and clothes, some things brought from Norway. Grandma slept in the brass bed between the south and west windows. My bed was back in the corner, behind the door. Above Grandma's bed was an oval gold framed picture of a little girl in a light green dress, sitting on the ground looking up at a singing bird in the branches overhead.

A while back, when browsing through an antique shop in Scottsburg, Indiana, I saw the very same print and a nostalgic feeling swept over me akin to pain. Tears pricked my eyes as I was transported back in time to my Grandmother's homestead bedroom. I resisted buying it. I reasoned that it was an unnecessary expenditure; I had no place to hang it, and I really did not need it. Later, I did go back to look at the picture again, but it was already sold.

Isn't it strange how a picture can evoke such sudden vivid memories long ago tucked away in the hidden recesses of your mind? It is strange how seeing a piece of fabric in an old patchwork quilt can give instant recognition of a garment worn over fifty years ago. In your mind's eye, you can once again recall how young and pretty you were then in this special dress. Or the sight and fragrance of a yellow rose brings memories of young love and the joy of receiving it; the song of a bird and the sound of the wind whistling around the window carries you back across the miles to a faraway place.

Next to Grandma's bed was an antique dresser and mirror. In the top small drawers were a few lovely pieces of antique jewelry. Fastened in the frame of the mirror was a white paper, on which was a beautiful black silhouette ink drawing with delicate detail of two lovebirds on a leafy branch, which Grandma said one of her children had made for her. Her daughters Edna, Estella, and Hilda were very artistic as well as my father, Henry.

Grandma Martha had a large Norwegian Bible she read from at night, and she recited the Lord's Prayer in Norwegian. She and Uncle Louie tried to help me pronounce some Norwegian words, reading from the Bible. Out of shyness and fear that I would make a mistake and appear stupid, I refused to practice or repeat the words, which I now regret.

Grandma had a nightly ritual of sitting on the edge of her bed and with her head bent low she would brush her long thick hair several strokes with a brush. Even in old age, her hair retained much of its dark brown color. In the morning, she again brushed her hair, and wound it on top of her head in a knotted coil secured with hairpins. She wore ankle-length dresses similar to the type she had worn years ago, rather than cater to modern styles of shortened skirts. Though her waist had thickened with age, and her face was wrinkled, I think she had once been beautiful with her lovely, wide, crystal clear blue eyes.

My grandmother was born March 19th, 1867 at Rush River Wisconsin, and was named Martha Helena Thompson. Rush River was about 5 miles from Baldwin, WI. She was the daughter of Haldor Bue Thompson, born in 1822, a timber worker and blacksmith who had come from Utne, Norway, an area known as Hardanger. If he had remained in Norway he would have gone by the name of Torbjurnson. But as a common practice among immigrants, a simplified spelling of their name was adopted. When Martha was four years old, and her sister Elizabeth was only a few months old, their mother died of fever. Martha also had a brother Tom. Their father married again about 1873. Martha at a young age was expected to do the work of a grown woman, putting in long hours and helping to raise her four half-brothers: Oliver, Helmer, Dick, and Christian.

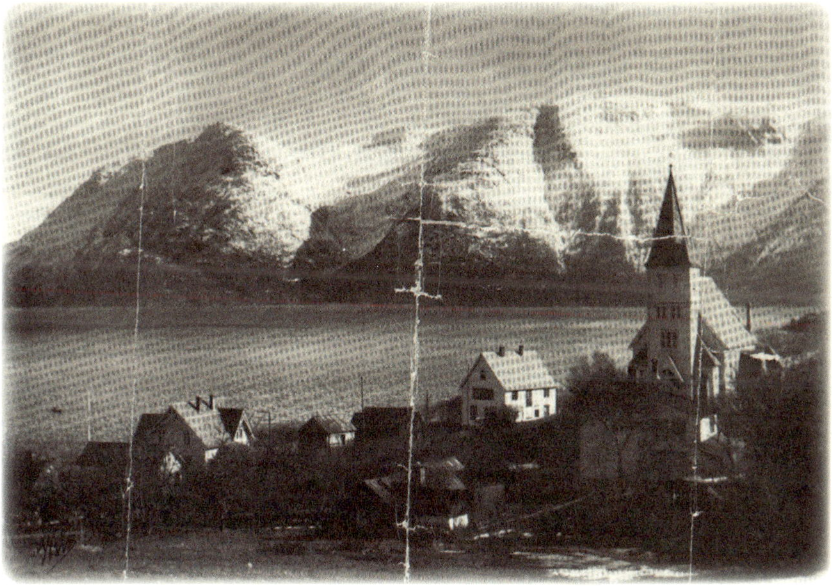

BIRTHPLACE OF HALDOR BUE THOMPSON
IN UTNE, NORWAY

As a young girl, Martha studied the Lutheran catechism, and she knew her Bible. In school, her teacher awarded her for high scholastic achievement, a framed needlepoint motto that said, "KNOWLEDGE IS POWER." Years later she hung this motto above the living room door that led to the kitchen in her North Dakota homestead cabin. When I graduated from Washburn High School as class valedictorian in 1954, Grandma Martha gave me money for a pretty pink graduation dress and told me I could have the motto "Knowledge is Power". Since I was going away to Asbury College in Wilmore, Kentucky, I didn't take it down off the wall. I thought when I had a home of my own I would get it then. To my regret, it burned with the old homestead cabin.

Mary A. Barnes Williams, a prominent early citizen of Washburn, North Dakota, personally interviewed fifty pioneer mothers who were married and lived there previous to statehood, November 1st, 1889. In 1922, she wrote a book entitled *Fifty Pioneer Mothers of McLean County, North Dakota*. My grandmother, Martha Helena (Thompson) Lorentzen is included in this wonderful book. From this book, I have discovered information about her to relate some of the highlights.

The story was told long ago that Martha, a young beautiful girl of 17, was at the spring drawing up a bucket of water when a tall, handsome Norwegian man with sandy hair and blue eyes came down the path to meet her and carried the water for her. He was Lorentz Lorentzen who had come to America on his father's ship **The Noah** and had worked his way down the Great Lakes. Hearing of a Norwegian settlement near Baldwin, Wisconsin, and possibly people he had known in Norway living there now, he had traveled to visit them. No doubt by this time he knew that his father, Captain Emanuel, the crew, and the ship ***The Noah*** were gone forever.

Martha and Lorentz were married on January 20, 1884 in Baldwin, Wisconsin. From there they went to Chicago where Lorentz worked on the shore of Lake Michigan as a shipbuilder and doing other jobs. They happily settled into an apartment that faced the lakefront. This life in the big city was very different from the country life Martha had known, but she was happy to be sharing a home with her young, sailor husband, whose jobs took him on trips to various cities on the Great Lakes for two or three weeks at a time. A precious baby girl, Elizabeth, was born to them on December 14, 1884. What joy she brought to them! Sadly though, a deadly plague of cholera infantum swept through Chicago after a summer of intense heat, taking hundreds of Chicago infants and their own darling nine month old daughter from them in September, 1885. What heartbreak this brought!

Grandma Martha told me that, while they were living in Chicago, they went to hear the noted evangelist, Dwight L. Moody, and they purchased a paper-back book of his sermons. Grandma in her later years gave this book to my sister Estell. I believe that under the preaching of Moody and reading his book that they learned of Christ's salvation for them and received Him as their personal Savior.

On the Lakes, Lorentz met a boat hand who worked on boats headquartered at Bismarck, North Dakota and traveled up and down the Missouri River. He told Lorentz of the free government land that was available there for homesteading. Although Lorentz had never been a farmer, he was very interested in acquiring this land. Martha's people, the Thompsons, had also already left the Norwegian community of Wisconsin and had gone west to McLean County in Dakota Territory. My great-grandfather, Haldor B. Thompson became the third homesteader in McLean County. In the spring of 1883 he filed a claim on 160 acres of farmland two miles north of Washburn.

In the spring of 1886, Lorentz and Martha decided they would also move west to join the Thompsons and others in the land of promise. There were tender signs of spring when they left Illinois. On finally reaching Bismarck, however it was cold with a raw, chilly wind sweeping over the brown, barren prairie. Patches of snow remained on the slopes of the hills. There were strips of blackened prairie where fires had swept across, exposing glacial boulders and bleached buffalo bones. Bismarck, with its straggling streets and a few buildings with shoddy, false fronts, looked desolate.

While Lorentz took the stagecoach to Washburn to find a place for them to live, Martha stayed in a hotel in Bismarck. She found the people there friendly and busied herself crocheting a chair tidy, which the hotel hostess admired so much that Martha gave it to her. In appreciation, the lady refused payment for Martha's stay there.

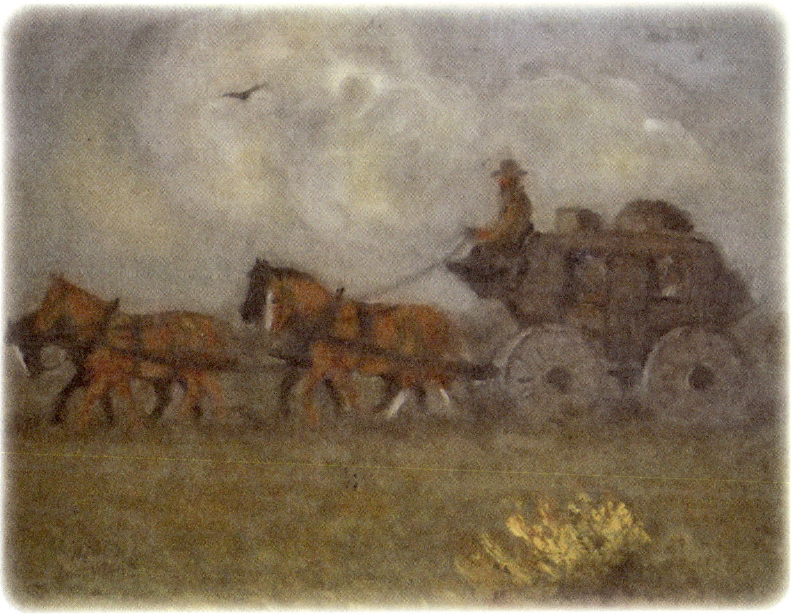

"STAGECOACH TO WASHBURN"
OIL PAINTING BY HENRY LORENTZEN

Lorentz returned to Bismarck with his father-in-law's team and lumber wagon to bring Martha and their household goods to her father's homestead. The trip from Bismarck to Washburn took two days. Along the way they stopped at a cabin, where they found the owners gone, but according to prairie hospitality they entered the unlocked door, brewed some coffee, and ate the lunch they carried.

After staying with the Thompsons a few weeks, they located a vacant shack, roughly built with planks, where they set up housekeeping in their first Dakota residence. Lorentz was away much of the time earning wages, so Martha, a young wife of 19, expecting a baby, was left alone much of the time. She was very lonely, missing young friends and another woman to talk with. Approaching storms, the thought of Indians, and the dark nights alone terrified her. She cried herself to sleep to awaken in the night, listening to mysterious sounds and the whistling wind around her crude shanty.

In the daytime for company, she sat on her doorstep entertained by the playful antics of little gophers. From her tiny window, she quietly watched a covey of prairie chickens that settled each day in the shade of the shanty. Her eyes hopefully searched across the endless prairie for the arrival of her husband or a visitor. She watched the billowing clouds drift across the blue sky, sometimes racing over the sun to cast moving shadows over the vast land. The prairie grass swayed and sighed in the wind. The song of the brave meadowlarks lifted her spirits.

That summer a cabin was built from a stack of logs piled near the shack. Part of the shack was torn down to complete the cabin. The last few nights in the old shack Martha slept without a roof over her head. The cabin was finished in time before the arrival in September of a baby girl, Edna Rosanna in 1886. What a joy and comfort she was for her parents to once again hold a sweet baby in their arms, after suffering the loss of their baby Elizabeth in Chicago.

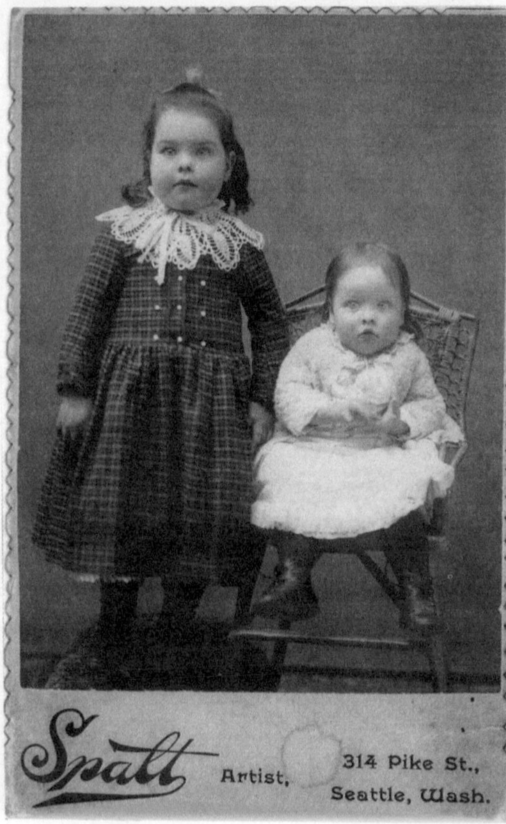

EDNA (LEFT) & ESTELLA (RIGHT)

Martha and baby Edna stayed much of their time alone on the prairie, while Lorentz was hired in Washburn doing carpentry work and painting. God was watching over them when a neighbor delivered a load of coal and unloaded it in the cellar just before a fierce, three day blizzard set in. They would have perished without this timely delivery.

In the following spring of 1887, Martha and baby moved into a better home to be a caretaker while the owner took work elsewhere. Lorentz continued to work in town. While this was a more comfortable home, there was much more work feeding the many travelers who stopped by, but there was less time to be lonesome.

Lorentz and Martha still had not acquired their own land since coming west, but they still desired to be landowners. They preempted or took over a homestead property that had been given up near Underwood. They moved into the comfortable sod house that was boarded up. They now owned a team of horses and three cows, but Lorentz was not a farmer and hired his farm work done while he continued to work in town. Here another baby girl, Estella Amelia, was born on July 28, 1889.

Work was becoming scarce and Lorentz grew restless longing for his old life on the waterfront. He heard of a boom on the west coast, so they gave up the preemption on the homestead after three years and left for Seattle. There Lorentz found immediate work on the docks with good wages. He also built boats and sold them. Here in Seattle, their fourth daughter, Hilda Christine, was born on October 7, 1891.

While they enjoyed the ease of living there, with its pleasant climate, an abundance of fruit and vegetables, and boating excursions and picnics on the beach, Martha longed for the simple life of the prairie, where they could own land and be near her family, the Thompsons. After three years or so, they returned to Dakota. In their absence, Dakota territory was now divided into two states, with Bismarck the capital of the north one.

For a few months, they lived in a small log house in Washburn and then bought a relinquishment nearby, where they lived for a few years. Their first son, Emanuel, was born there on June 24, 1895 with only his father to assist. Louis appeared on the scene two years later on December 5, 1897. Martha was kept busy caring for their five children, overseeing work while Lorentz continued to work in town.

One summer day, Martha made a trip by horse and buggy to the wooded bottomland along the Missouri River to pick berries. She passed an unoccupied log cabin located at the mouth of the Buffalo Paunch Creek on the Missouri River about three miles above Washburn. The view from the cabin was beautiful, overlooking the woods and the Missouri River with distant, square-topped buttes just beyond. She told her husband Lorentz about it. This led to the purchase of this property, obtaining rights to a 160 acre homestead. At last, their dreams and longing for ownership of their own land was fulfilled. Their wandering over land and sea came to an end as they happily settled down to live there the rest of their lives. Three more sons were born, Henry on July 11, 1900, Haldor on October 20, 1902, and Osborne on June 20, 1905.

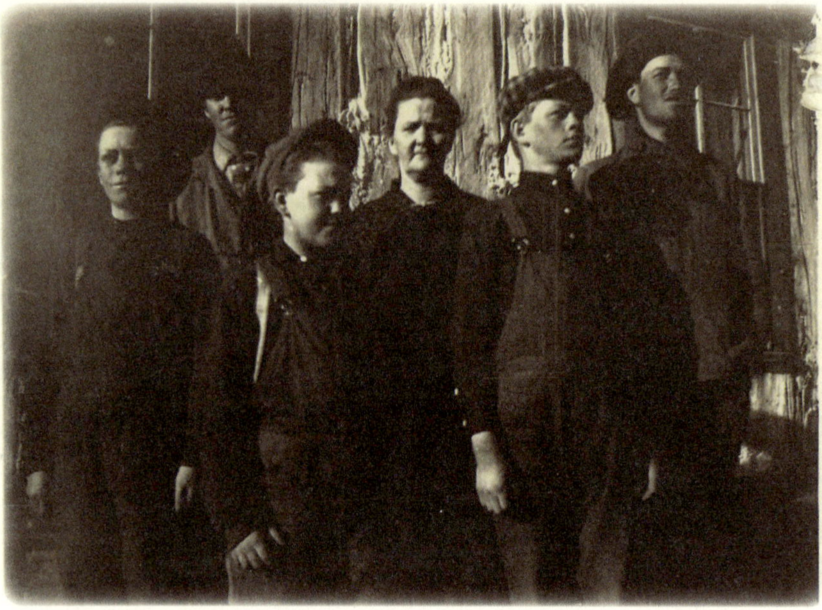

HALDOR, EMANUEL, OSBORNE, MARTHA, HENRY AND LOUIE

Everything seemed to be going well for the Lorentzens until that fateful day in November 1906, when Lorentz suffered a stroke of paralysis and died so unexpectedly at the young age of 56. Martha, left a widow with eight children, continued to live on their homestead, raising cattle and horses and cultivating the fields with the help of her sons.

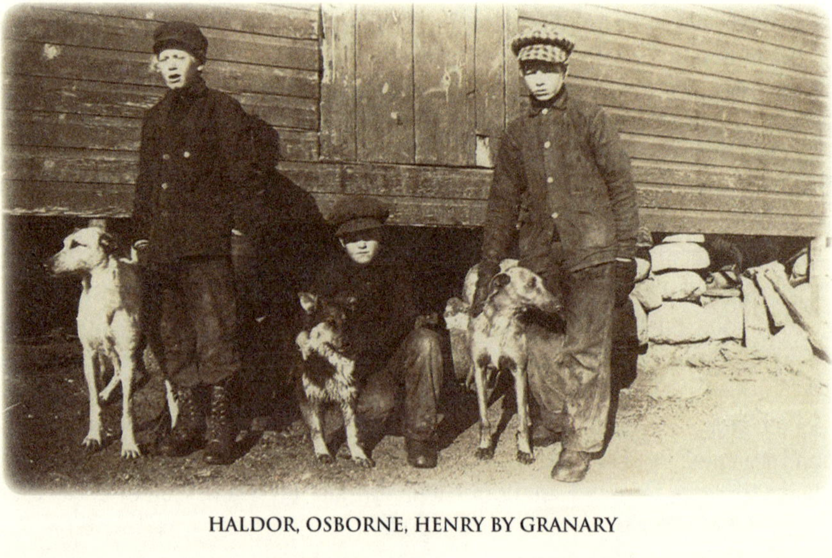

HALDOR, OSBORNE, HENRY BY GRANARY

Within the next three years, Martha was to experience more sorrow. Her father, Haldor B. Thompson, died in June 1909 at the age of 87 and was buried in St. Olaf's Cemetery south of Turtle Lake, North Dakota. No one was prepared a month later for the tragic death of Martha's daughter Edna at the young age of 22 on July 4, 1909, buried in the Riverview Cemetery at Washburn, not far from her father Lorentz's grave.

In our walk through the rooms of the old Lorentzen homestead cabin, I don't recall seeing any musical instruments, but the family was musical and sang well without accompaniment. My father sang portions of the national anthem of Norway in Norwegian, and several songs that were popular during World War I and in the 1920's, such as "How You're Going to Keep Them Down On the Farm?", "Yes, We Have No Bananas Today", and " After the Ball Is Over".

When I was a kid, my folks had a portable phonograph or record player – a victrola – in a case that spun large black records around on a turntable. A crank handle had to be turned or "cranked" sufficiently to wind up a spring or some mechanism inside the case. An arm holding the phonograph needle was then lowered onto the record. On the phonograph was the RCA logo or symbol of a large megaphone with a terrier dog sitting facing in front of it with his head and ears cocked forward listening. I think this record player had been my father's while he lived in the homestead before he married. My brothers and sister and I liked to listen to it and sing along with the slightly quavering voices on the old records.

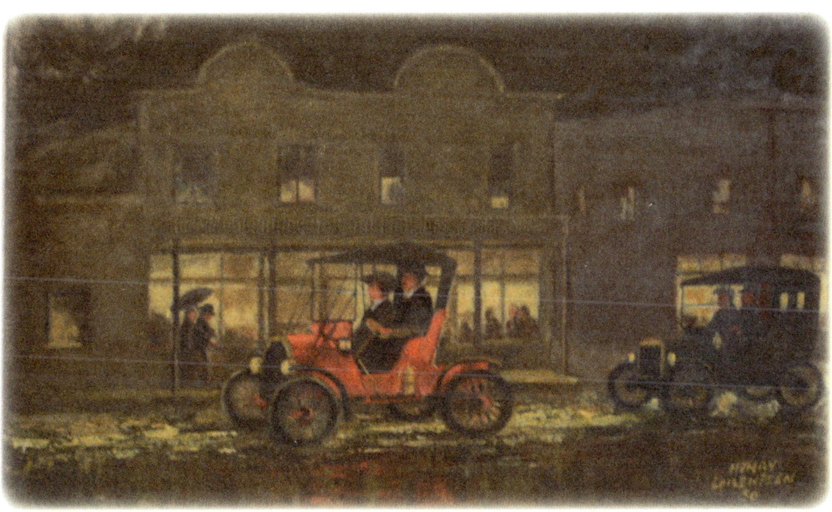

"WASHBURN STREET"
OIL PAINTING - HENRY LORTENZEN

In the 1920's before my parents married, young people drove for miles from scattered farms on the prairie and from nearby towns to attend house parties, or an occasional barn dance which was their main opportunity for socialization. It was at one of these parties my mother Grace and father Henry met. Blanche, my mother's older sister was at the party with Osborne, my father's youngest brother. Their courtship led to a double wedding near Brandt, South Dakota on September 27, 1931. The Barlow sisters married the Lorentzen brothers.

My Uncle Osborne and Aunt Blanche lived for several years near White Earth, North Dakota, so we didn't see them very often. They taught in one-room schoolhouses, and raised paint horses-- the old strain of spotted Indian horses descended down through the centuries from the full-blooded Arabian horses brought from Spain to Mexico.

They had three sons, Lorentz, Lee, and Leslie. It was always an exciting time when they, our double cousins, came down to visit us. We children had fun playing "Cowboys and Indians". My father recalled how amusing it was to hear Lorentz say, "Yipes! The white men are attacking our village!" as he ran around the house.

I have a memory of my Uncle Osborne standing in our living room in the little white house where we lived on the farm my folks had bought in 1944 that adjoined on the east the old Lorentzen homestead. He had on a cowboy hat and boots, and wore a nice western cut jacket and pants. It must have been at our request he sang some popular western songs of maybe Jimmy Rogers, Ernest Tubb, or Hank Snow. He sang with a deep voice of confidence, his feet braced apart, and his head thrown back. He must have passed on his love of singing and music to his son Lorentz who in turn passed it on to his large family. I remember the summer of 1972 when my husband Byron, our children and I visited my

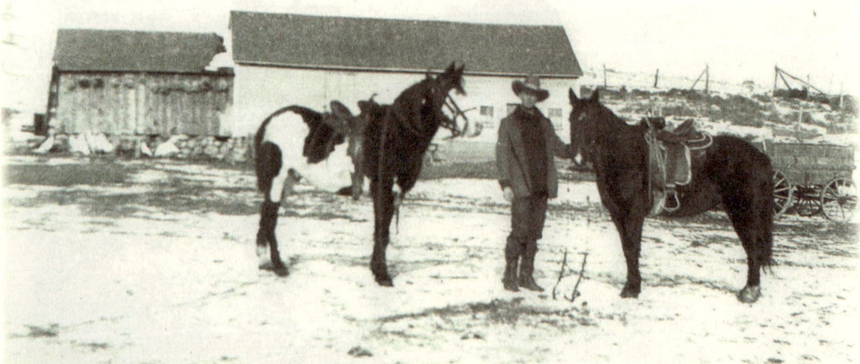

OSBORNE BY HOMESTEAD GRANARY

childhood home in North Dakota. My cousin Lorentz and his wife Mary Lou and their children arrived from Canada in an old school bus they had fixed up for traveling. Lorentz had his family sing for us which sounded good. Their son Tim played the guitar which he now continues to play and sing with his children. It is good to see talent passed down from one generation to another.

Uncle Osborne and Aunt Blanche, when their sons were grown, moved to Montana to raise paint horses and live on a ranch their son Lee was buying. So several years went by without my seeing them. Uncle Osborne died there in 1975 of cancer. In September 2013 while traveling with my daughter Martha and her husband Mike Munchhof in Montana, we stopped in St. Ignatius where we found the graves of Uncle Osborne and Aunt Blanche far from their North Dakota roots.

Just west of the old Lorentzen homestead, my Uncle Haldor and Aunt Mabel lived not far away with their children, Richard, Karen, Edna, and "Little" Haldor. We had good times playing together in their hills and coulees. Aunt Mabel was a gracious hostess serving us a delicious lunch of her home-canned peach sauce and baked treats. Uncle Haldor also liked to sing some of the old country-western songs heard on the radio and had a nice voice. Uncle Haldor, born in 1902, had special mechanical ability to keep the farm machinery running, such as the old threshing machine and tractor in time of harvest, and other equipment and vehicles. This talent he passed on to his sons and his love of music and singing to his daughters. He passed away in 1988.

I wish I had known all my father's sisters and brothers well. My father appreciated and valued all the members of his family, even distant cousins, and tried to keep in contact with them. His sisters Edna and Estella died before I was born, and others lived so far away that I seldom saw them. Hilda was married to Robert (Bob) Bryson and lived in the state of Washington. I remember she came by train a couple of times to visit her mother Martha and her brothers. As a young woman, Hilda was ahead of her time by acquiring a camera

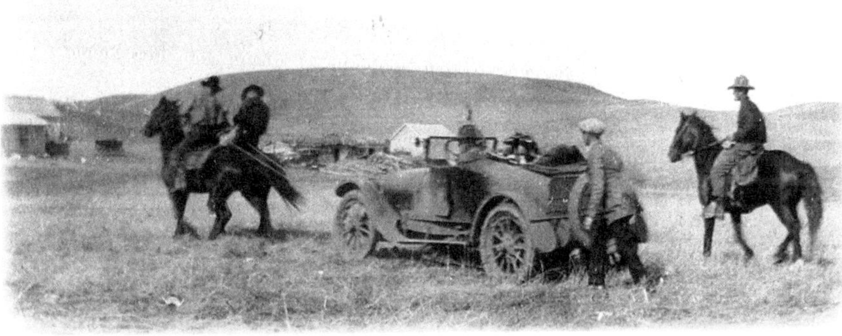

and taking photographs that had negatives made on thin, rectangular pieces of glass, and she developed her own pictures. She had an artistic eye for capturing dramatic poses of her brothers and their horses. Her photography was perhaps influenced by the old black-and-white movies of the cowboy star Tom Mix. Because of Hilda's photography, we are blessed to have some of her photos in this book.

My father said that his sister Hilda was a great encourager for him to continue his artwork. I've not had the opportunity to meet her children since they lived on the West coast, but my father wrote in a note saved among his old papers that she had five children: Helen, who died at about age four, Eunice, Grant, Lucille, and Virginia. My father's sister Estella was married to John Jasmann, and they lived near McClusky, N.D. She died at the young age of fifty. She had two daughters, Camille and Ruth who never had any children, and two sons Leslie and Mike who married and settled near Ennis, Montana with their families.

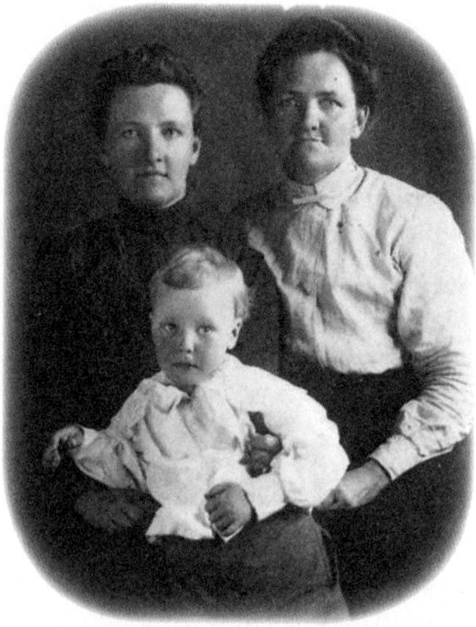

SISTERS ELIZABETH (LIZZIE) LARMER
WITH SON JOHN JAMES
& MARTHA LORENTZEN

Grandma Martha's younger sister Elizabeth, who was a baby when their mother died in Wisconsin, came to North Dakota with their father, Haldor Bue Thompson and their stepmother Regina Valasvaard. She met and married James (Jim) Larmer who came from Ontario, Canada. They settled in the White Earth, North Dakota area. My father Henry, when a young man, spent time visiting the Larmers and recalled good times with his aunt Lizzie and her family there. In the summer of 1930, he helped build a cabin for the Larmers. In my father's keepsakes is the picture of his mother Martha sitting with her sister Elizabeth (Lizzie), who is holding her son, John James Larmer, born on March 30, 1910. Aunt Lizzie too was a hardworking, brave pioneer wife and mother who has an unwritten story.

The old homestead place, chosen by Lorentz and Martha, has remained in the Lorentzen family for over 100 years. The old log home with all its family treasures is gone, but the memories still live on. Lorentz and Martha's grandsons, Richard and Haldor Junior, and a great-grandson Cody (Haldor Junior's son), continue their labors there, building upon the dream that brought Grandfather Lorentz and Grandmother Martha to this prairie land of promise in the west so long ago.

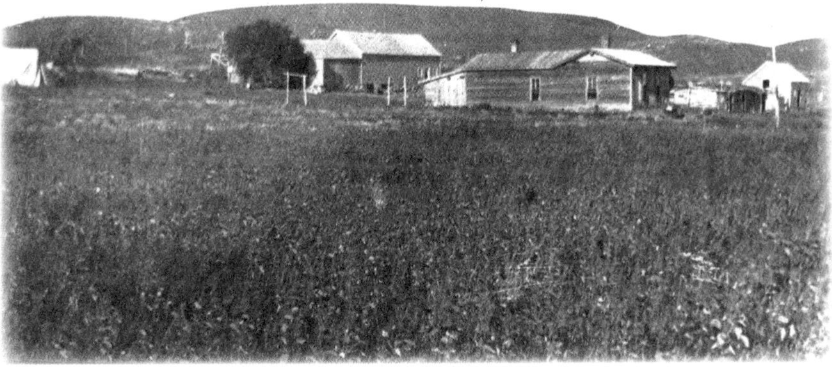

LORENTZEN FAMILY HOMESTEAD

The writing of this story has revealed so many sorrowful happenings my grandparents endured in their lifetime: the death of Captain Emanuel and the crew on ***The Noah***, the death of Martha's mother when she was four years old, the death of Lorentz and Martha's first baby girl, Lorentz's early death, the death of their beautiful daughter Edna and her baby, and about thirty years later the death of their daughter Estella.

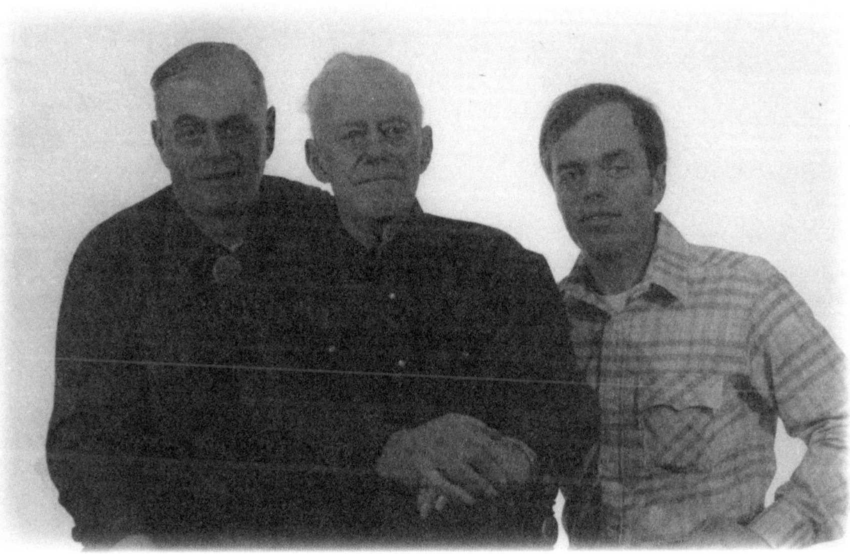

UNCLE HALDOR WITH SONS RICHARD AND HALDOR JUNIOR

It seems that all this tragedy would be nearly unbearable, but I believe that Grandma Martha must have found strength and help from God. I like to believe she bravely stood beneath the dome of the North Dakota blue sky, hearing the song of the meadowlarks, and raised her eyes to the prairie hills to say, like the psalmist David: *"I will lift up mine eyes unto the hills, from whence cometh my help. My help cometh from the Lord, which made heaven and earth."* - Psalm 121:1

If it were known, there is within the life of every human being a story that could be written. Everyone in their lifetime will experience a variety of happenings or events, some that will be told, and some that are silently stored away behind closed doors of the heart and mind, and not talked about. In a life, there will be times of hardship, sadness, sorrow, disappointment, maybe even bitterness and regret; but hopefully there will be times of love, happiness, joy, contentment, forgiveness, and victory.

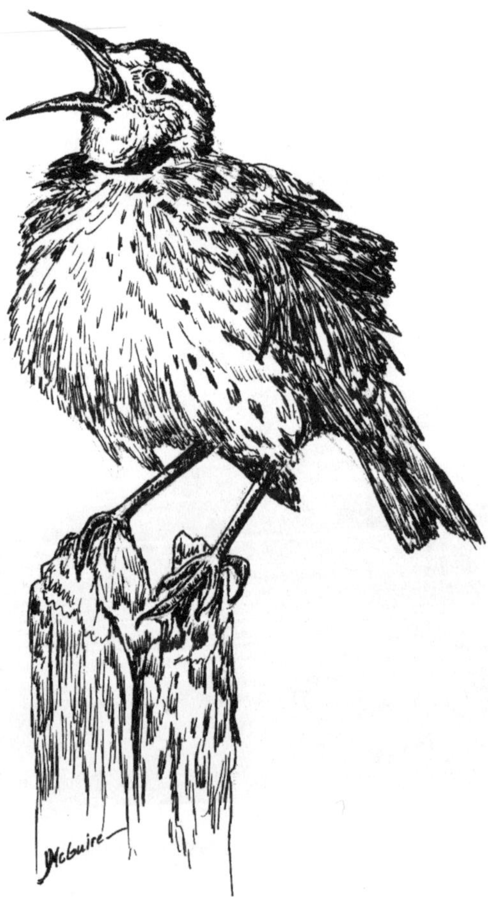

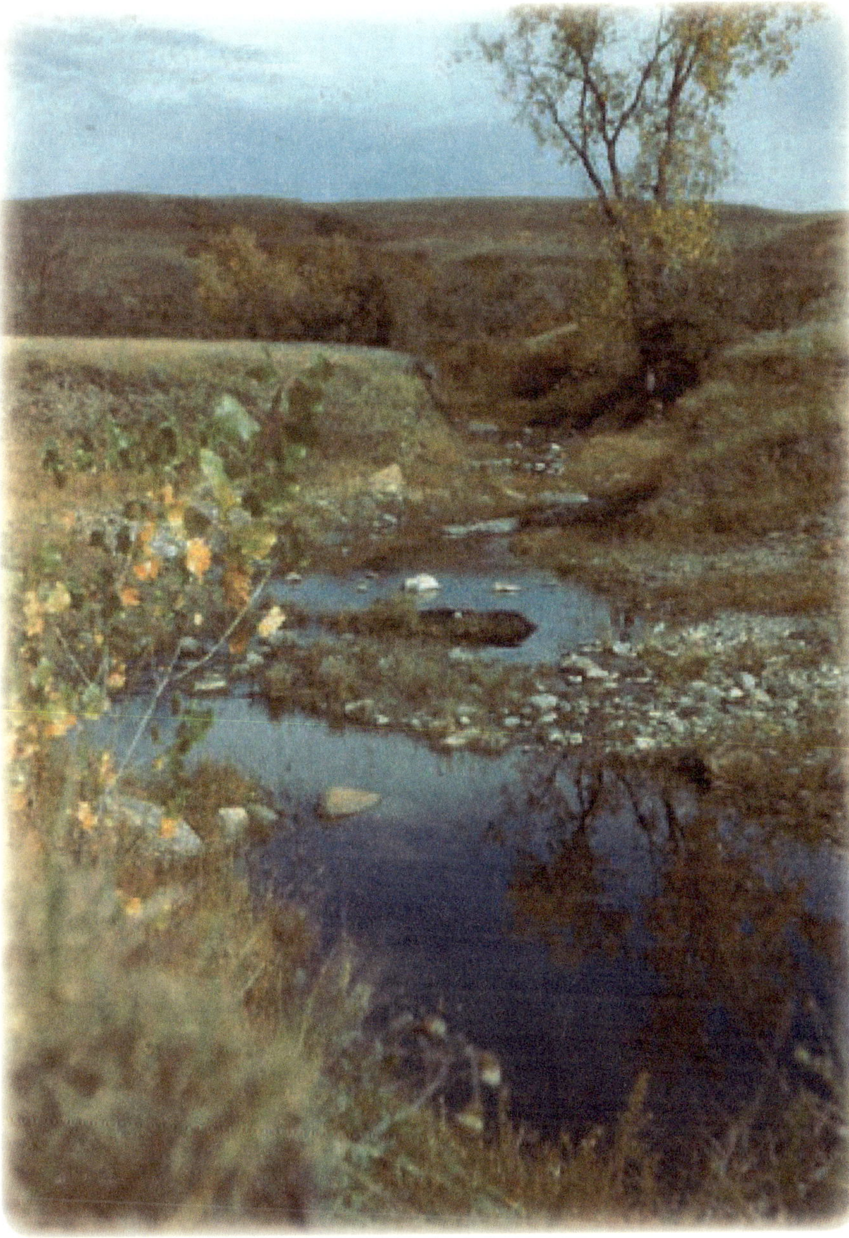

THE BUFFALO PAUNCH CREEK
ON THE LORENTZEN HOMESTEAD

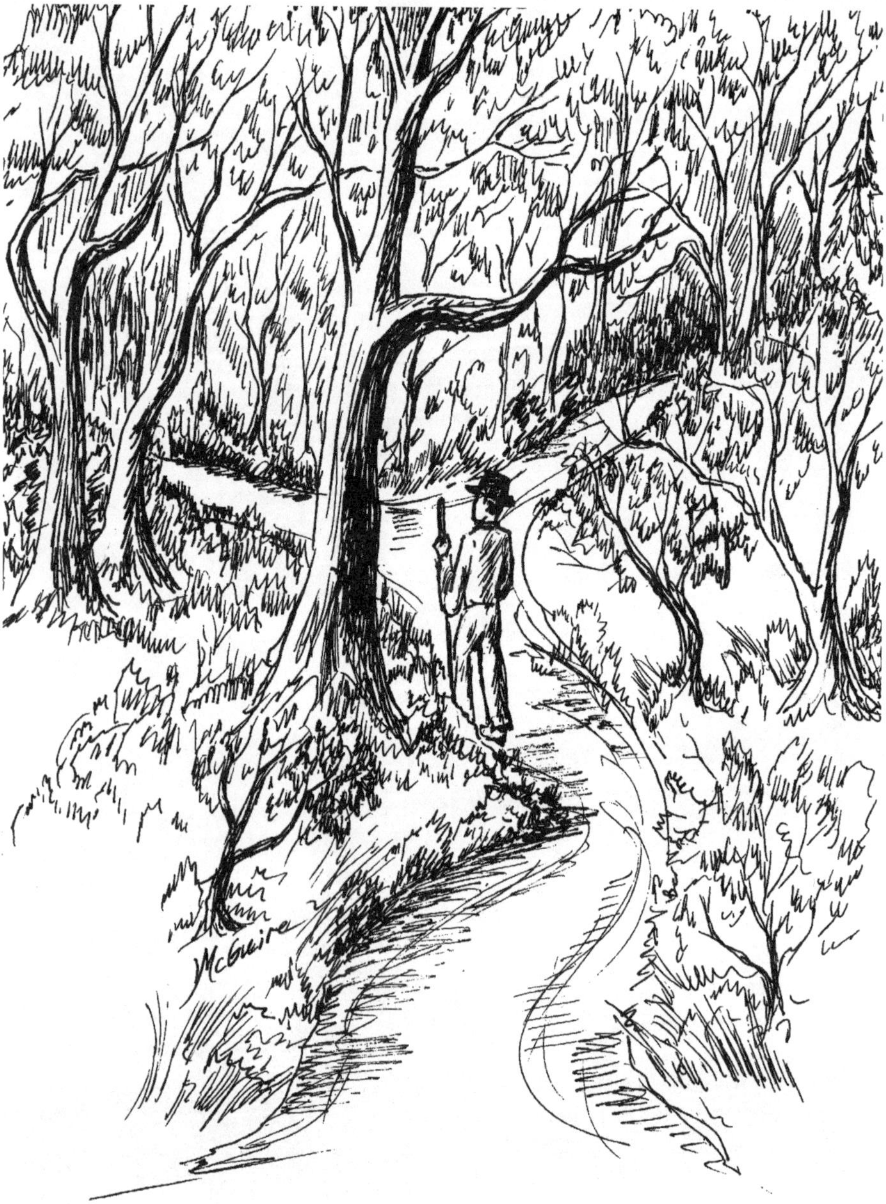

"WHICH WAY SHOULD I GO?"
PEN & INK DRAWING BY YVONNE MCGUIRE

CHAPTER 10

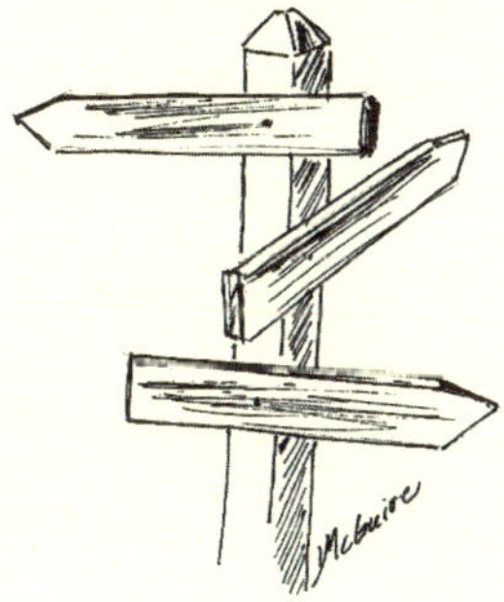

Choices and Decisions

The summer of 1952, the time of helping my grandma Martha came to a close. I have a vivid memory of a day in August when I stood on a hill behind the homestead cabin looking across a sea of rippling grass to the distant horizon of prairie hills meeting the wide expanse of sculptured white clouds adrift in a cobalt blue sky. A feeling came to me out of nowhere, like a revelation borne on the prairie wind, that somehow my future would take me beyond the horizon of those sheltering hills that encircled my little world there.

My entire summer had been spent with grandma and my uncles, Emanuel and Louie at the homestead without the company of school friends, without going to town, and only very briefly seeing my family. My folks told me the news that a new pastor, Reverend James MacKay, and his wife, Reva, had come to the Methodist Church in Washburn. With them was a foster girl my age, Margaret Holmes. She would be in my class. The MacKay's were graduates of Asbury College in Wilmore, Kentucky. In the school year of 1952-53, I began regularly attending church, and taking part in the youth meetings with Margaret. In the MacKay's and Margaret, I saw their love for the Lord and their personal relationship with Him. That year held special significance for me. I was to make the most important decision of my life.

On the evening of February 15, 1953 at the Methodist Church, I responded to the invitation to receive Christ as my personal Savior. I went forward to kneel at the altar as we sang "Where He Leads Me, I Will Follow". Praying there, I received assurance that Christ had come into my heart and life, and my sins were forgiven. He gave me a new joy and a desire to serve Him and truly follow Him wherever He may lead me.

By my senior year, I felt God wanted me to go to Asbury College. Margaret planned to go there. By trusting God that He would somehow provide, I applied to Asbury and was accepted for the fall of 1954. God miraculously met my needs. By studying hard and receiving high grades, I was awarded a scholarship from the Johnson Wax Foundation in Racine, Wisconsin. I also worked in the college cafeteria, and received some help from my folks and a few anonymous donations. So, my four years of college were paid for by the time I graduated with honors – magna cum laude – in 1958. Grandma Martha, who as a school girl in Wisconsin, diligently studied to earn the needlepoint motto, "Knowledge is Power", would have been proud of me. While at Asbury, I met and married my husband, Byron McGuire from southern Indiana, son of Francis and Louis (Hansen) McGuire. Byron also had made the decision to receive Christ into his life and had felt God leading him to Asbury College and into service for Him.

In my college days, my folks did not have a telephone. Of course there were no modern means of communication like e-mail and cell phones, which families today daily use to keep in touch with loved ones. So the nine-month school years would go by without seeing my family or hearing their voices. We wrote weekly letters which took a few days to receive. I was very lonesome and missed my family and my North Dakota home very much. When the mail arrived at the college post office, there was always a rush of students anxiously opening up their mailboxes.

I will always remember going to the post office on a day in March 1956 and happily seeing I had a letter from my mother. Byron happened to be with me, though we weren't engaged at the time. We walked to a bench out on the campus lawn and I opened my letter. My happiness turned to sorrow, as I read the news that my grandma Martha had died and was buried shortly before her 89th birthday. Tears filled my eyes and I regretted that I wasn't able to be there. I remembered my dear pioneer grandmother who so bravely endured hardship, pain, and sorrow in her own life, but did not complain but was a blessing to others, an example to future generations.

As I look back on my family heritage and the people who have greatly influenced my life, I'm in awe of God's providence. Over the years I've saved a clipping I took from the March 1992 issue of Reader's Digest, entitled

"What a Background!" It reads as follows:

> *"Next time you're feeling rather unimportant, try a little arithmetic trick based on the undebatable fact that it took two people, your parents, to get you here. Each of your parents has two parents, so in the generation just prior to that of your mother and father, there were four people whose pairing off and sharing love contributed to your existence. You are the product of eight great-grandparents, 16 great-great grandparents, 32 great-great-great-grandparents, etc. Keep on multiplying the number by two. If you figure an average of about 25 years between each generation, you'll discover that a scant 500 years ago, there were 1,048,576 people on this planet beginning the production of you."*
>
> -The Rev. Gene Britton in East Point, Ga., Southside Sun

I marvel at God's creation, His unsearchable riches, power, and wisdom. We as individuals had nothing to do with the choices of our parents, their ancestors, and our birth, but God knew all about us from the beginning. Psalm 139:13-17 expresses so well the mystery of life:

> *"For Thou hast possessed my reins:*
> *Thou hast covered me in my*
> *Mother's womb.*
> *I will praise Thee; for I am*
> *Fearfully and wonderfully made:*
> *Marvelous are thy works; And*
> *That my soul knoweth right well.*
> *My substance was not hid*
> *From Thee, when I was made in secret,*
> *And curiously wrought in*
> *The lowest parts of the earth.*
> *Thine eyes did see my substance, yet*
> *Being unperfect; and in Thy book*
> *All my members were written,*
> *Which in continuance were*
> *Fashioned, when as yet there was*
> *None of them.*
> *How precious also are thy thoughts unto me, O God!*
> *How great is the sum of them!"*
>
> -Psalm 139:13-17

We can ask ourselves many "what if..." questions. What if my grandfather Lorentz Lorentzen had decided to return to Norway with his father, Captain Emanuel Lorentzen on ***The Noah*** to be lost at sea instead of deciding to stay in America? This whole story would not be written, because I would not exist.

We can think of multiple choices we have made that have affected the course of our life and the lives of others. It has been my desire through life to seek and to do the will of God. Sometimes the will of God is not clear to us, and sometimes, though we may know what God would want, we deliberately choose to go our own way. How important decisions are! Making a choice to go or stay, or take the road to the right or to the left, can make all the difference in the world, influencing generations to come.

Robert Frost, noted American poet, wrote the following poem about coming to a fork in the road in the woods and choosing the road to take.

The Road Not Taken

Two Roads diverged in a yellow wood,
And sorry I could not travel both
And be one traveler, long I stood
And looked down one as far as I could
To where it bent in the undergrowth;

Then took the other, as just as fair,
And having perhaps the better claim,
Because it was grassy and wanted wear;
Though as for that the passing there
Had worn them really about the same,

And both that morning equally lay
In leaves no step had trodden black.
Oh, I kept the first for another day!
Yet knowing how way leads on to way,
I doubted if I should ever come back.

I shall be telling this with a sigh
Somewhere ages and ages hence:
Two roads diverged in a wood, and I-
I took the one less traveled by,
And that has made all the difference.

- Robert Frost

Wouldn't it be wonderful if we could be so in tune with God's leading for our lives that we could always choose the right path to follow? Isaiah 30:21 says: "and thine ears shall hear a word behind thee, saying, this is the way walk ye in it, when ye turn to the right hand, and when ye turn to the left." Similarly, Jeremiah 42:3 assures us of the following: "That the Lord thy God may shew us the way wherein we may walk, and the thing that we may do."

Despite our wrong choices and lost opportunities or failures to correct it, by the help and grace of God we can experience a new life and hope in Him. When we receive Christ as our Savior, we can claim the promise in 2 Corinthians 5:17, "Therefore, if any man be in Christ, he is a new creature, old things are passed away; behold, all things are become new."

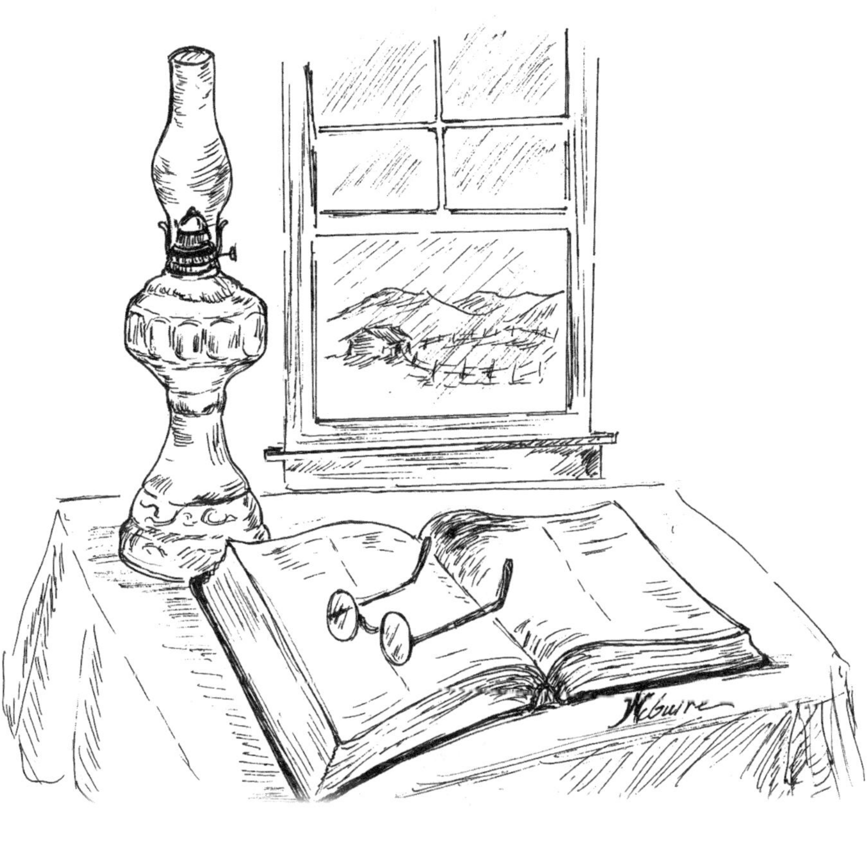

Acknowledgements

I want to thank the many who have been an encouragement and a help to me in the writing of this book. Several who read my first book, "Daddy Was an Artist", have told me they are looking forward to reading this book which has kept me pressing on when at times I considered giving up and quitting.

I am especially thankful for the following:

- Henry Lorentzen, my father, who had a lifelong commitment to preserving our family history and portraying pioneer living on the prairie in his numerous paintings.

- John Lorentzen, my nephew, who values his grandfather Henry's art work and his collections of old notes, letters, news clippings and photos to share with me.

- Amanda Lorentzen, John and Darcy's daughter, whose interest in history and research was very helpful in my writing about the notorious Bassanella brothers who came to Washburn in the early 1900's.

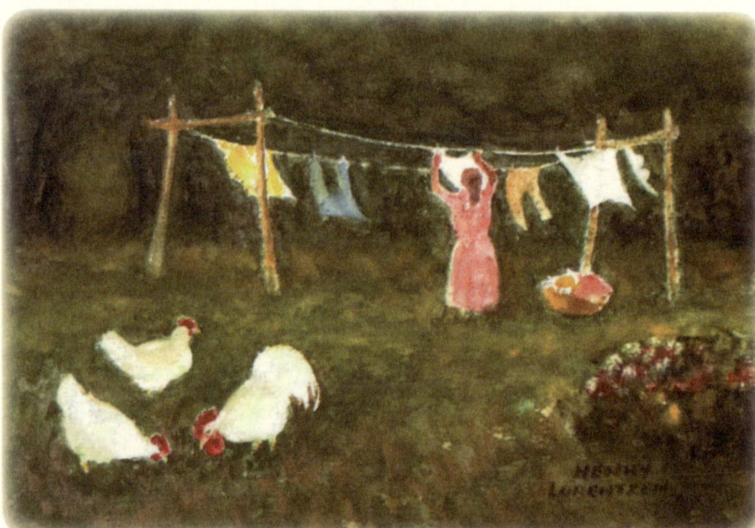

OIL PAINTING BY HENRY LORENTZEN

Acknowledgements

• Norman and Ross Lorentzen, my brothers, my sister Estell Torgerson, and cousin Karen Lorentzen who shared their memories with me.

• Vanessa and Tim Lorentzen, my niece and nephew, and their daughter Starlit Lorentzen who have been very helpful in scanning photos, typing and emailing information.

• Martha Grace Munchhof, my daughter, who has encouraged me and given valuable suggestions in reading my manuscript in its various stages.

• North Dakota friends and family who have shared Henry Lorentzen paintings from their private collections to be photographed for illustrating this book.

• Aunt Hilda (Lorentzen) Bryson, my father's sister, whose photographic skill in the early 1900's provided old photos in this book.

• Harry Kesselring, North Dakota friend and neighbor, photographed the Lorentzen Farm shown on pages 54 and 55. His daughter Coleen Schulz generously made her father's wonderful photos available to us.

• Wesley Torgerson, longtime North Dakota friend, whose beautiful scenic photographs are on pages 16,31,47, and 93

• Cierla McGuire, my granddaughter, and New Life International intern and friend, Steven Opperman, for patiently and skillfully typing my manuscript.

• Duvon McGuire, my son, for his encouragement and writing the foreword to this book.

• Stephanie DeBoer, owner of DeBoer Creative, LLC., Byron's and my great-niece, who artistically designed the layout of this book.

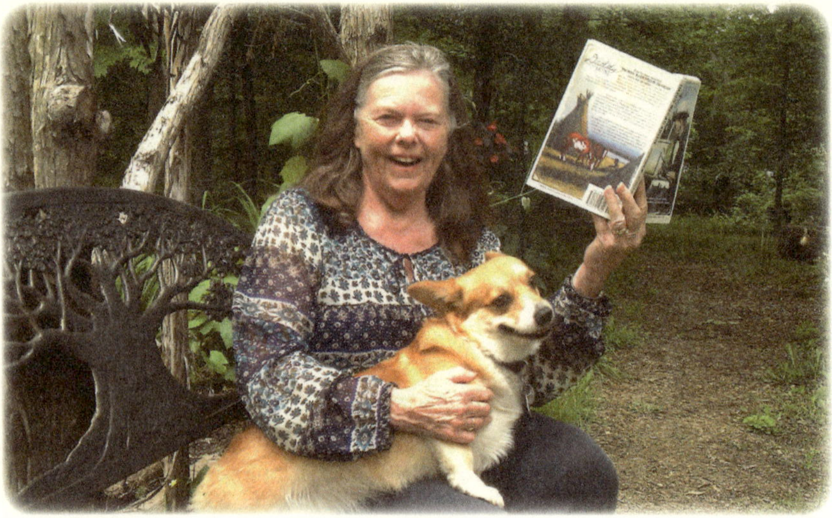

YVONNE MCGUIRE
WITH HER WELSH CORGI, FOXY